information
NATION

information
NATION

Education and Careers
in the Emerging Information Professions

Jeffrey M. Stanton,
Indira R. Guzman,
and Kathryn R. Stam

Information Today, Inc.
Medford, New Jersey

Second printing, February 2012

Information Nation:
Education and Careers in the Emerging Information Professions

Library of Congress Cataloging-in-Publication Data

Stanton, Jeffrey M., 1961-
 Information nation : education and careers in the emerging information professions / Jeffrey M. Stanton, Indira R. Guzman, and Kathryn R. Stam.
     p. cm.
 Includes bibliographical references and index.
 ISBN 978-1-57387-401-4
 1. Information science--Study and teaching (Higher) 2. Information scientists--Training of. 3. Information science--Vocational guidance. 4. Information science--Study and teaching (Higher)--United States. 5. Information scientists--Training of--United States. 6. Information science--Vocational guidance--United States. 7. Information technology--Study and teaching (Higher) 8. Information technology--Vocational guidance. 9. Library education. 10. Library science--Vocational guidance. I. Guzman, Indira R., 1967- II. Stam, Kathryn R., 1966- III. Title.
 Z668.S73 2010
 020.71'1--dc22

                                                                    2010023157

Cover Designer: Shelley Szajner   **www.infotoday.com**

The publication of this work was supported in part by a grant from the National Science Foundation to the first author. The National Science Foundation does not necessarily support any of the findings or conclusions presented in the work.

To Judy, Abe, Arlene, and Walter—JMS

To Rita, Miguel, Indira Jr., and Margaret—IRG

To Terrin, David, and Deirdre—KRS

Contents

Acknowledgments

We would like to express a simple thank you to the people who helped us with this endeavor. This project traces its roots back to 2001, when we first met at the School of Information Studies at Syracuse University. Since then, each of us has been teaching and learning about the information professions in one form or another. This effort to share what we have learned was supported by the National Science Foundation's (NSF) IT Workforce program, which partially funded the research reported in this book with award CNS-0420434 to the first author. We would like to note that the NSF does not necessarily endorse any of the findings or conclusions of this book.

Collection and organization of data reported in this text would not have been possible without the efforts of Isabelle Fagnot and Debra Eischen, who both played a pivotal role in conducting interviews and focus groups. We also thank Shuyuan Ho, Aaisha Haykal, Jonathan Reed, Mike Leotta, Tyler Blanchard, George Ellis, and Raed Sharif for their assistance with myriad research tasks. The School of Information Studies at Syracuse University, first under the leadership of Raymond von Dran and later under Elizabeth Liddy, hosted much of the work that went into this project and provided numerous opportunities to discuss the ideas in this book with students, faculty, and university staff. The SUNY Institute of Technology's School of Arts and Sciences has also been helpful by facilitating our access to student volunteers. TUI University's Colleges of Business Administration and Information Systems provided support and access to students and faculty who participated in discussions about this book and provided useful ideas.

We are so grateful to all of the research participants, including IT students from Syracuse University, IT professionals from a wide variety of central New York organizations, and volunteers from all over the country who contributed through StudyResponse. Some of the chapters in this book refer to outside experts, and we thank them, especially Ron Foster, Jill Hurst-Wahl, and Susan Skrien, for sharing their thoughts about librarianship with us. The writing process has been considerably easier due to the assistance of Deirdre Corcoran, who helped us rescript several important themes after her initial reading and editing of the book. We are also grateful to our families for their support throughout the process. Thank you, all.

Introduction

Just one generation ago, information technology (IT) was expensive and complicated. If you wanted to create new information technology, you had to be a specialist with years of training and special aptitudes. IT people were "geeks" and "nerds," a strange class of too-smart people with minimal social skills who were paid top dollar to stare at a screen and tap at a keyboard for hours every day. Enrollments in computer science, computer engineering, and information systems majors were growing, and the allure of good money attracted students of all stripes who had hopes of mastering the arcane internal logic of the central processing unit.

Then came the infamous dot.com bust of 2001. Newspapers and magazines widely reported that all of those high-paying jobs building computers and writing software were going overseas. IT and software development had become low-wage activities (too cheap to meter), and few American college students would bother to expend so much mental effort on developing the skills needed for a job that no longer existed in U.S. companies. Enrollments in computer science and related fields plummeted. U.S. students, especially women, essentially disappeared from technical majors in favor of occupations with more promise and glamour and less math and science. The geek and the nerd, always maligned, now also skulked off to the unemployment line, while low-paid workers from other countries took over their jobs. People across the U.S. were texting each other at flight speed, but you didn't need to major in computer science to master the controls on a flip phone.

Fast-forward a few years, and it seems that the outsourcing fear mongers have gotten it wrong. Information and the technology that manipulates it are now central to the conduct of nearly every profession in which the U.S. plays a leadership role: management, finance, accounting, product development, architecture, engineering, aerospace, medicine, agriculture, meteorology, and many others.

Although memory chips and MP3 players are commodity items whose unit price is diving precipitously toward $0, this trend does not apply to the complex IT infrastructure that supports industries such as pharmaceutical research, transportation, banking, insurance, and energy management. In these industries, technology has accelerated the use of information but has simultaneously opened up a Pandora's box of complexity and challenges. Although you can purchase a personal computer at your local department store for less than the cost of a plane ticket, large companies still collectively spend trillions of dollars every year on running their information systems and paying the staff that analyzes, develops, and deploys them. Where is all this money going? In 1897, Mark Twain famously wrote, "[T]he report of my death was an exaggeration." Perhaps the death of the American information worker is also an exaggeration. The lowly geek of the pre-internet age has become transformed into a new class of specialized expert: the information professional.

So who are these information professionals? Are they the system architects, software project managers, network engineers, information assurance specialists, digital librarians, or IT support staff? The answer is yes, all of the above. Is technology all they do? The answer is definitely no. While technology is a vital feature in the life of the information professional, it is only half of the story. The other half is the "user," a very small word for the very large collaborative and organizational challenges surrounding the use of information and technology. Organizational science, psychology, anthropology, and communications play an increasing role in system design and architecture and are as integral to the information professional's work as the technology itself. Experts now believe that effective use of information technology depends at least as much on the insights of these social sciences as it does on computer science and engineering. Today's information professionals can no longer afford to learn just the technical or engineering details; they must instead develop the ability to understand human information and collaboration needs, capabilities, and limitations at the individual, group, and organizational levels.

There is an astonishing gap in public understanding of both the activities and challenges of work in the information professions. Mention the phrase *information professional*, and many people stare back at you with a blank look. Few seem to adequately grasp the idea that a librarian, systems analyst, network manager, database developer, and CIO are all working on different facets of the same essential underlying challenges. Almost every aspect of human life in our part of the world—food, energy, water, safety, health, money—depends upon the information that flows through a sophisticated infrastructure of networks and databases, computers, and software. Most critically, understanding the challenges, excitement, and, yes, even glamour of the information professions has not yet caught hold of the American psyche, and as a result, there is a shortage of U.S. workers with the skills, creativity, and entrepreneurial spirit to ride the global wave of information innovation.

To make matters worse, many current U.S. college students seem both ill-prepared and disinterested in participating in the new information professions. The Organisation for Economic Co-operation and Development (OECD) conducts an international study of student achievement every few years.[1] The most recent report, published in 2006, shows that the U.S. ranked about 30th in math and science achievement among the developed countries of the world, below Latvia, Croatia, and Poland, among others. Students in U.S. colleges mistakenly equate their ability to use cell phones, text messaging, Facebook, and World of Warcraft with a subtle understanding of how to design, build, support, and sustain a complex information infrastructure that has utility and value for a profitable enterprise (Grant, Malloy, & Murphy, 2009). Those students who are lucky enough to get jobs in such businesses often find that they are not equipped with the skills needed to succeed. Part of the problem is that traditional academic majors are poorly suited for training information professionals. Computer science, mathematics, business, psychology, anthropology, economics, political science, education, and design have each ascended into their own stovepipes with little regard or appreciation for what is happening elsewhere on campus. Yet a mixture of the skills and knowledge represented in each of these different majors is exactly what a contemporary student needs in order to become a valued and valuable contributor to solving an organization's information problems.

Of course, no book would be complete, after a litany of doom-and-gloom propositions such as these, without a proposal or a solution. Fortunately, a new educational focus is emerging in some institutions. These schools are taking an interdisciplinary approach to educating tomorrow's information professionals by mixing together science, technology, social science, and design. These new programs are beginning to educate students in these new professions—not as programmers or coders or software developers, but as professional analysts, architects, and creators of our planet's critical information infrastructure. This book describes findings and conclusions from a three-year research program on the information professions, highlighting the barriers to inclusion and to retention of U.S. students in information-related majors. The book also describes and analyzes the forces that are preventing high school and college students from getting the interdisciplinary skills they need to help the U.S. regain and retain leadership in the world of information. The solution proposed by this book, then, is education, but education in a mode that is only beginning to emerge from the shadow of traditional approaches. Read this book if you want to learn what everyone needs to know about the new class of professionals who will control the future of information and technology. Read this book if you care about the competitiveness of U.S. students in the global competition to control one of the most complex and valuable resources in our world: information.

Endnotes

1. Executive summary of the full report available at www.pisa.oecd.org/dataoecd/15/13/39725224.pdf.

References

Grant, D. M., Malloy, A. D., & Murphy, M. C. (2009). A comparison of student perceptions of their computer skills to their actual abilities. *Journal of Information Technology Education, 8,* 141–160.

CHAPTER 1

Wanted: Information Professionals

Do not follow where the path may lead. Go, instead,
where there is no path and leave a trail.
—Ralph Waldo Emerson, American poet

The U.S. Department of Labor's Bureau of Labor Statistics (BLS) exists for one reason: to find out what is happening in the U.S. labor markets. The BLS spends nearly $600 million of U.S. taxpayer dollars per year doing this, and its reports provide a more comprehensive and unbiased view of the recent, current, and future labor situation in the U.S. than any other single source. The BLS does not always get its predictions right, but it has more sources of data and a longer historical perspective than any other group that tracks labor trends. In the November 2007 Monthly Labor Review provided by BLS, the occupation projected as the fastest growing in the U.S. for the period of 2006–2016 was "Network systems and data communications analysts." In the BLS occupational projections report from November 2009, this job was listed as the second fastest growing position in the U.S., with 53.4 percent growth expected by 2018 and wage growth projected as "very high."

Some quick facts on this employment category include a 53 percent projected growth in the number of positions, a salary designation of "very high" (the topmost category), and a bachelor's degree as the necessary training. Yet the U.S. Department of Education reported the most popular college major as business, with 312,000 degrees awarded in the most recently available full-year reporting period, 2004–2005 (2008 data continue to show business as the most popular major, comprising 16.4 percent of all undergraduate degrees). Business schools offer many majors, from finance and accounting to entrepreneurship, but marketing is often popular among students, particularly those who see themselves as having poor math skills (Pritchard, Potter, & Saccucci, 2004). What does the BLS say about the prospects for marketing majors? Of course, a business graduate may use the degree in a number of different positions. But if a person chose a position such as "Advertising and promotions manager," which is a likely job for some marketing majors, the growth projected by the BLS for the decade between 2006 and 2016 is just 6.2 percent, with an average of only 1,300 new and replacement jobs opening up nationwide per year across the entire country. A recent search of a major internet job advertising site revealed 439 full-time positions across the U.S. for the title "Events/promotional marketing" as opposed to 2,518 job openings for "Systems analyst" (a title commonly used for information technology professionals in business contexts). With deep apologies to friends and colleagues who teach in marketing departments, it seems that marketing majors may have to plan on spending some serious time in the unemployment line (Brady & Davis, 1993; Kelley & Bridges, 2005; Reibstein, Day, & Wind, 2009).

There is a bit of mystery surrounding the reason some college students choose to major in fields where limited job growth opportunities seem to be the rule rather than the exception. Why major in one of these limited growth fields when most of the new high-paying jobs over the next 10 years are likely to be in information systems, healthcare, and educational services (Dohm & Shniper, 2007)? While marketing is an area of study that is interesting and an essential profession to businesses, it *should* matter to students if the job growth potential in marketing is low relative to other professions. If college students are thinking carefully about their futures and their prospects for staying gainfully employed in a turbulent world, their decisions about which major to pursue does not seem to reflect this thought process clearly. Does the country need 300,000 new undergraduate business majors per year, while enrollments in various science, technology, engineering, and math (STEM) majors continue to drop across the country? A U.S. Department of Commerce Report (Mitchell, Carnes, & Mendonsa, 1997) showed that both women and African Americans, in particular, seem to shy away from participation in the information technology workforce (as well as several other science and engineering areas). Could it be that students are choosing a major and a profession based on faulty information—about the world of work, the future of our society, job markets, their own proclivities, or all of the above? Or maybe colleges and workplaces have created situations that make women and underrepresented minority students feel unwelcome. Could it be that educators, parents, guidance counselors, or the media are somehow discouraging students' pursuit of technology education as well as other nationally important areas such as science, engineering, and math?

Here's a working hypothesis: The answer is yes to all of the above.

Let's take a closer look at some ideas that might support or refute our hypothesis. Students may have faulty information about working in the information field or other high-growth areas. Where do they get their information? Friends, parents, television, YouTube, Facebook, Wikipedia, teachers, and/or guidance counselors. Using these sources, do high school students and college freshmen get a realistic understanding of what it would be like to have a career in technology as a network systems and data communications analyst, for example? And if students have an unrealistically rosy expectation about the potential of a profession, such as criminal forensics, where did they get those ideas? Perhaps students believe that the network systems/data communications analyst job involves sitting in a dark cubicle in front of a flickering computer screen all day or inhaling fumes while soldering circuit boards or running cables through dusty basements and crawl spaces. If students think that these activities describe the jobs in the information field accurately, they may not make good decisions in choosing a major and profession.

Let's also ask where people think the U.S. is heading economically. It would be valuable to have a better understanding of why jobs are being moved from the U.S. to various countries around the world and why certain jobs are affected more than others. When the economy is bad and many people are losing their jobs, which industries are robust against the downturn? Some skills learned in college provide a flexible foundation for lifelong learning and adaptability and allow a worker to move easily from one career to another when necessary, while other skills learned in college only work in one kind of job. What are these flexible, foundational skills?

What is happening in the economies and labor markets of countries such as India and China, and how will these changes affect workers in the U.S.? Hidden inside the details of a 2007 BLS report is the statistic that computer programming is the only job on a list of 30 professional occupations that is likely to experience an employment decline over the next 10 years in the U.S. (Dohm & Shniper, 2007). How can the outlook for the information profession be so bright overall when the job that people equate most closely with information technology—computer programmer—is likely to experience a decline? The only way to figure this out is to get a subtler understanding of the following key questions:

- What makes it possible to outsource a job?
- What happens to the previous jobholders when a job gets outsourced?
- How can people in outsourced jobs be prepared to reinvent themselves?
- What kinds of jobs are unlikely to be made obsolete by new technology or turned into low-wage positions?

We also need to look in the classroom, both in college and before college. What do students learn about the value of math, science, technology, and engineering? Perhaps the way we teach math and other "hard" topics has little relation to the way people use math in the workplace and elsewhere.

Finally, we need to talk to the students themselves. We should try to get a clear understanding of how they see their careers and what skills they have, especially in math and science, but also with respect to other areas such as psychology or sociology. Do these skills match the demands of the information professions? Given the demands of jobs such as network systems/data communications analyst, we want to know if high school seniors or college freshmen are prepared well enough to be successful—first in the major itself and later in the profession. If colleges can remediate any existing skills deficits, we want to know if we can then recruit students into information-related majors with the promise of getting them up to speed.

That's a lot of difficult questions. To lead rather than follow in the world economy, however, the answers to these questions hold critical importance for the future. Collectively, we are facing some major difficulties: climate change, financial meltdowns, declining availability and increasing cost of fossil fuels, water shortages, poverty, piracy, extremism, and epidemics. Only a few resources really matter going forward into the decades. Energy, raw materials, technology, and clean water are undeniably important, but the force that levers these resources into powerful and sustainable economic engines is people working together to solve problems. Information is the linchpin resource for solving problems. Information professionals are the experts in managing this resource, but the quality of education in science and technology provided recently has not been great. In a 2006 report produced by the nonpartisan, international Organisation for Economic Co-operation and Development (OECD), U.S. students ranked as low as 35th in science proficiency and as low as 36th in math proficiency. In both of these cases, the U.S. ranked substantially below our economic competitors such as Korea, the U.K., and Germany. One out of every four U.S. high school students failed to exceed the minimum level of proficiency in science.

We are unlikely to maintain global leadership if this situation persists. We need more individuals whose education has helped them develop sophisticated technical skills and knowledge, particularly in areas of high demand and complexity such as the information professions.

While energy, transportation, and environmental engineering are also important, the growth of each of these sectors is accelerated by information technology and those who design and deploy it. We need innovators who can recognize a societal problem and develop a cost-effective, resource-preserving solution.

In this book, we examine why the U.S. is not producing enough of these innovative, technology-savvy professionals and what we can do about it. We focus on the information professions—including information technology, information science, computer science, telecommunications, and related areas—because these professions help to create economic and societal value across most areas of human endeavor. We focus on undergraduates because an undergraduate degree provides the best point of entry into the job markets for information professionals. Some but not all of what we say is applicable to other areas of technology and engineering, but we don't possess or claim expertise across the entire spectrum of fields and technical professions. Nonetheless, there is information here that could be valuable for students, families, and others who are concerned about choice of major and choice of career regardless of their areas of interest.

We have organized this book into three major sections. First, we take a broad look at business, government, the military, and other enterprises across the world to see how information is transforming almost every human activity. In these chapters, we examine what outsourcing really means and its effects on those nations that gain and lose jobs. This section also takes a closer look at the information industry itself and how a variety of forces have made our global information infrastructure at once more accessible to more people and more complex than ever. If you want to know how the U.S. arrived where it is right now, read this section first.

In the second section, we dispel the myths and describe the facts about what information professionals do. By providing a realistic overview of the diversity of jobs under the information umbrella, we believe that we can begin to address the questions related to the image and attractiveness of the various jobs in the information professions. In several of these chapters, we hear about the information field from those who are studying it in college and those who are involved in it at work. At the end of this section, you will know more about the information professions. If you want to understand the everyday life of a student or worker in the information fields, read these chapters.

In the final section, we look forward to the future and try to understand how the world of education, especially higher education, can successfully educate the next generation of information professionals. While this book contains no silver bullet for fixing the country's higher education system, we offer some straightforward actions that parents, students, guidance counselors, and educators can take to get us back on the right path. We believe that local, practical improvements can add up to significant important change at the national level over time. And while we are quickly falling behind other countries, there is no time like the present to start to catch up.

References

Brady, J., & Davis, I. (1993). Marketing's mid-life crisis. *The McKinsey Quarterly* (2).

Dohm, A., & Shniper, L. (2007). Occupational employment projections to 2016. *Monthly Labor Review, 130*(11), 86–125.

Kelley, C. A., & Bridges, C. (2005). Introducing professional and career development skills in the marketing curriculum. *Journal of Marketing Education, 27*(3), 212.

Lacey, T. A., & Wright, B. (2009). Occupational employment projections to 2018. *Monthly Labor Review, 131*(11), 82–123.

Mitchell, G. R., Carnes, K. H., & Mendonsa, C. (1997). *America's new deficit: The shortage of information technology workers.* www.eric.ed.gov/ERICD ocs/data/ericdocs2sql/content_storage_01/0000019b/80/14/ff/a4.pdf. Retrieved July 7, 2009, from www.technology.gov/reports/itsw/itsw.pdf

Pritchard, R. E., Potter, G. C., & Saccucci, M. S. (2004). The selection of a business major: Elements influencing student choice and implications for outcomes assessment. *The Journal of Education for Business, 79*(3), 152–156.

Reibstein, D. J., Day, G., & Wind, J. (2009). Guest editorial: Is marketing academia losing its way? *Journal of Marketing, 73*(4), 1–3.

PART 1

Information Is Changing the World

These chapters put the information professions in context by justifying how information is used, showing how technology development has become simplified, and outlining why certain information profession jobs are difficult to outsource. Chapter 2 discusses the problem of information proliferation and uses this to justify why we need the information professions. Chapter 3 discusses how different professions now require the use of information and information technology. This chapter provides a detailed example using the science of biology to show how information technology has changed this science. Chapter 4 discusses how information technology development, including software development, has undergone a kind of democratization that gives access to greater numbers of people with less training. Using an analogy from manufacturing, the chapter illustrates how as underlying technologies become more modular, new "mash ups" are consequently easier to develop. Finally, Chapter 5 uses the insights from Chapter 4 to demonstrate the way outsourcing and offshoring change industries, using as a concrete example the shoe manufacturing industry in Brockton, Massachusetts.

CHAPTER 2

Information Wants to Be ... Disorganized

We are drowning in *information*, while starving for wisdom. *...

—E. O. Wilson, Harvard biologist

Cryptography is a branch of applied mathematics that deals with transforming information to and from a secretive form. Cryptography provides the basis of many of the essential services available on the internet today. Online shopping sites provide a prime example: Without cryptography, it would be very difficult to send credit card numbers and other sensitive information securely across the internet. One early development in cryptography was published by Italian architect and author Leon Batista Alberti (1404–1472) in about 1466 (Gille, 1970, pp. 96–98). The method he developed, called the Alberti Cipher, was remarkably advanced for its time, no doubt because Alberti himself was such an accomplished thinker. In the 1400s, the realm of human knowledge was sufficiently small, so that a talented individual such as Alberti could become an expert in science, mathematics, architecture, archeology, education, finance, and other areas over a normal lifetime. That era in history was dotted with notable individuals such as Copernicus, Galileo, and da Vinci, who had mastered a significant proportion of the human knowledge available in Western civilization at the time.

Notably, this era was also the time of Johannes Gutenberg, inventor of the movable type printing press, which played such an important role in the diversification and distribution of human knowledge. With sufficient wealth during this age, an individual could possess a library of nearly every book available to humankind, and the number of available books was sufficiently small so that a dedicated individual could actually read them all. Thinkers of this early Renaissance age must have found it uniquely satisfying to have such a broad understanding of so many areas of knowledge, while also working on the cutting edge of unexplored scientific and mathematical terrain.

Such a broad-based mastery is impossible in the present day. Futurist and visionary technologist Ray Kurzweil has estimated that developing expertise in an area of endeavor requires memorizing a minimum of 100,000 "chunks" of knowledge. In this context, a chunk of information refers to an interconnected package of facts or ideas that you can think about in a single thought. For instance, if you want to scramble an egg, you have to have a hot pan, some oil, a bowl to hold the raw egg, a fork to scramble it, and a spatula to turn the egg in the pan. You can keep all of this data in your brain at one time; this one chunk of information consists of several facts and a procedure. Because you've learned, practiced, burned some eggs, and practiced some more, you have a cohesive package of information in your head about scrambling an egg, and you can reliably cook this most basic of breakfasts. If you wanted to extend this tiny bit of learning into becoming a full-fledged professional chef, you would have to master thousands and thousands of additional tasks, activities, skills, and knowledge areas, not only in food preparation but in purchasing raw materials and tools, managing a kitchen staff and restaurant finances, maintaining sanitation and hygiene, and so forth. A quick scan of current books in print shows more than 85,000 books about food, 46,000 books about cooking, more than 1,800 books about becoming a chef, and nearly 1,200 books about restaurant management. Many people spend years getting educated and working in apprenticeships to accumulate this knowledge. The sheer volume of information available makes it extremely challenging to achieve mastery even in this one quite focused area of professional practice.

The plentitude of written knowledge about this single area of endeavor demonstrates a well-documented trend in human knowledge: Increased specialization leads to increased proliferation of information. In turn, this proliferation leads to further specialization as individuals master and extend what their predecessors have discovered. Eventually, it becomes difficult for one expert to speak to another expert because the terminology, concepts, and practices in one area no longer overlap with another. Although the cryptographer may be capable of scrambling an egg, he has little other common ground with the chef in terms of the professional knowledge and experience each possesses: You could choose to become a chef, or you could study the mathematics of cryptography, but it is exceedingly unlikely that you will do both at the mastery level. Even the cryptographers are highly specialized among themselves. The call for papers for the 2009 International Conference on Applied Cryptography and Network Security included 14 distinct topical areas on which submitted papers might focus. That conference was one of more than a dozen annual meetings where cryptographers might present their work. The mind strains to comprehend the amount of information continuously generated by people around the world. Researchers in the field of *scientometrics*—the measurement of scientific communications (Mabe & Amin, 2001)—have estimated that the amount of existing scientific knowledge in the world is currently doubling every 21 years. In contrast, the groundbreaking scientometric author Derek Price (1965) estimated that scientific knowledge took the 200 years between 1400 and 1600 to double in size.

In short, present-day information creation by the people of our world constitutes an embarrassment of riches. We literally have more information than we know what to do with. Information replicates faster than rabbits, and while we have plenty of hutches where the information can live, the continuous process of keeping all of that information organized has become overwhelming. Our favorite search engine companies have hired armies of researchers, technology developers, information architects, and other experts, and yet we have not come close to containing the flood. Dutch graduate student Maurice de Kunder created a website, WorldWideWeb Size.com (www.worldwidewebsize.com), that estimates and tracks the number of webpages in the world. On the day this paragraph was written, the estimate was that the web contained no fewer than 25.67 billion pages, each page having a distinctive uniform resource locator (URL), typically a long string of names beginning with *http*. That number of pages is more than triple the number that was present just 2 years ago. Yet your favorite search engine is likely to have indexed only 10 percent to 30 percent of that estimated total. In other words, a search engine cannot find or refer you to at least 20 billion of the webpages currently in existence. If you spend some time searching webpages for useful information, you might also agree that even those pages that *are* indexed—and are therefore available in search results—are sometimes poorly organized and often fail to deliver the fact, discussion, or information that you really wanted to see. We have more and more information available to us, but the information becomes more and more disorganized as we go.

Here's a little test that illustrates the point. Think back to the last time that you bought a new computer for yourself or for someone in your household who previously had one. Give yourself a gold medal if you were able to transfer every piece of user-generated information from the old computer to the new computer in one move, such as dragging and dropping the "My Documents" folder onto a writeable DVD. If you did this with confidence that you moved everything, you are a truly gifted information organizer. Give yourself a silver medal if you found everything you needed on the old computer and moved it piece by piece to the new computer in less than an hour. You get a bronze if you were able to do it in one afternoon. You get no medal at all if you're an "information disorganizer," like most of us, and you kept the old computer around for months or years afterwards because you were never quite sure that you had gotten all of the files, photos, videos, bookmarks, customizations, settings, backups, applications, project data, and so forth taken off the old machine. Even on this simple task of keeping our personal electronic files organized, we must make an enormous and continuous effort to avoid descending into information chaos. The problem is magnified hugely for governments, corporations, and nonprofits, which must keep their information organized to survive.

Once upon a time, in the kinder and simpler world of the past, we had a group of information organization experts who helped us remain in control of our knowledge and information. They were—and still are—called librarians. The public face of librarianship—the stereotypical conservatively dressed, middle-aged lady saying "shhh" (there's even a librarian action figure available at internet novelty shops that does this)—has generally obscured the more complex reality behind the scenes. For every public librarian checking out books at the counter or answering questions at the reference desk, we have a thousand working behind the scenes in academic libraries, corporate libraries, special libraries, government, and nonprofits, trying to keep the petabytes[1] of information in our modern world organized and accessible. (To keep things in perspective, the information stored just in academic libraries around the U.S. comprises about 2 petabytes.) In the back rooms of these various organizations, there have always been experts at information classification, evaluation, and organization who labored in relative obscurity to make sure that the materials available to library users were of the best possible quality and presented in an organized, predictable fashion.

For better or worse, the job has become far too big for librarians alone. In the middle of the 20th century, as electronic computers began their exponential rise into every nook and cranny of life, computer scientists began to realize that the manipulation, sorting, and indexing of information were complex problems that required extensive research. Information scientists—these are some of the experts who train librarians—determined that a critical component in the organization of information was *metadata*, the electronic offspring of the old-fashioned card catalog. Simultaneously, engineers began to devise equipment that could communicate, store, and process digital information at higher and higher speeds as well as more and more cheaply. These different streams of work converged in 1973 and 1974 when U.S. computer scientist Vint Cerf published a design for the internet. Over the next two decades, hundreds of scientists and technologists expanded this basic design into a globally interconnected communications system. The beauty and promise of the internet is that nobody owns it and everybody can contribute to it. In 1989, the invention of the World Wide Web by British computer scientist Tim Berners-Lee ensured that the internet's capabilities could be used for sharing multimedia information with anyone, anywhere, anytime, transcending the barriers of time and space with digital technology. Few anticipated that the result would be information chaos, but the 26 billion webpages and many petabytes of other data created by humanity so far are, for the most part, unstructured, disorganized, hard to find, or unreachable in many cases—an unmitigated clutter of good, bad, and indifferent data, unready to serve the many challenges we face.

This chaos is not always evident on the surface. You may routinely have success searching for and finding a favorite webpage for news, sports, or entertainment. But information users in business, government, healthcare, and education are frequently frustrated by the web's lack of structure, classification, archiving, security, veracity, timeliness, and ease of use. Here's a hypothetical scenario that makes the point: Imagine you have to start taking a new drug to help treat a serious medical condition you have. Although your pharmacist tells you that the drug does not interact with other medications you are taking, you would like to do some research to make sure. Choose between the following two possibilities: You can search the web yourself, or you can ask a medical reference librarian for help finding the most trustworthy and up-to-date materials. Searching the web yields 37,000 hits, comprising a random mixture of drug company marketing materials, swear-by-it testimonials, and overwrought horror stories reported by various people who have used the medication, cheery articles from popular magazines, and a two-sentence stub on Wikipedia. In contrast, within two minutes, the medical librarian helps you locate the full-text publication of the most recent peer-reviewed, large-scale clinical trial and provides a glossary for interpreting the medical terminology that appears in the article. If you went with the more sensible and reliable option of working with the materials selected, classified, and managed by the medical reference librarian, then you opted for professionally organized information instead of information chaos.

By its nature, information is disorganized, and it takes concentrated effort to keep it organized and ready for optimal use. The enormity of this task means that we need many more information professionals than we currently have. Another implication, though, may be that every educated person needs to become a bit of an information professional themselves, even if their real profession is in medicine, business, engineering, government, or education. Information literacy has become a "cross-cutting" skill that has become central to success in many endeavors much as more traditional kinds of literacy—reading, writing, and arithmetic—became essential in ages past. In a brief but stunningly prophetic article in 1959, novelist C. P. Snow said, "It is very stupid to attempt to make everybody into technologists; but it is essential that everybody, including the technologists themselves, should understand something of the intellectual and human meaning of what the technologists are all about" (Snow, 1959). Substitute *informationist* for *technologist*, and you have grasped the essential motivation for this book. Information is a literacy—knowledge, skills, abilities, and attitudes—that has become essential in every profession (as well as other aspects of life). The next chapter considers this idea in more detail by examining how information has begun to revolutionize areas that we haven't traditionally thought of as computational or informational.

Endnotes

1. A petabyte is 1,000,000,000,000,000 (one quadrillion) bytes.

References

Gille, B. (1970). *Dictionary of scientific biography.* New York: Charles Scribner's Sons.

Mabe, M., & Amin, M. (2001). Growth dynamics of scholarly and scientific journals. *Scientometrics, 51*(1), 147–162.

Price, D. J. D. (1965). *Little science, big science.* New York: Columbia University Press.

Snow, C. P. (1959). Two cultures. *Science, 130*(3373), 419.

CHAPTER 3

Doctor, Lawyer, Scientist, Chief: Every Profession Depends on Information

I find that a great part of the information I have was acquired by looking up something and finding something else on the way.
　　　　　　　—Franklin P. Adams, American journalist

Roger Arliner Young was an African-American scientist and, despite the unusual first name, a woman (Sullivan, 2002). Young published her first scientific article in 1924. In 1940, she became the first African-American woman to earn a doctorate in zoology with a dissertation titled "The Indirect Effects of Roentgen Rays on Certain Marine Eggs" (Manning, 1989). During the four decades from 1924 until her death in 1964, Young taught and conducted research at several small colleges in North Carolina, Texas, Mississippi, and Louisiana. In those years, zoology—and particularly marine zoology—was largely a descriptive science. The microscope was the most expensive tool most zoologists could expect to use in their research, and new discoveries arose from painstaking, repetitive, detailed efforts to detect, observe, and describe large and small organisms. The research reported in Young's dissertation likely required hundreds of hours' worth of handwork culturing the eggs of small marine animals, subjecting them to varying doses of X-ray radiation, and recording the results in a handwritten lab notebook. Computers as we know them today did not exist in 1942, although engineers at Harvard University were busy wiring up the five-ton Mark I electro-mechanical computer for its 1944 debut. Scientists conducted most calculations and all record keeping on paper using a trusty pencil and a slide rule. No working lab scientist anywhere in the U.S. or the rest of the world would get an opportunity to use a computer in scientific work for at least another 10 years.

Fast forward to the present, and we find scientists such as biologist Agnes A. Day, PhD, chair of the Department of Microbiology in the medical school at Howard University. Day and many of her fellow biologists routinely use gene sequencing tools to conduct their research (Day, McQuillan, Termine, & Young, 1987). A gene sequencer is an intricate marriage of biochemistry, digital photography, and computing. Genetic material sampled from the cells of any organism undergoes an ingenious progression of chemical transformations wherein each step is precisely timed and controlled by a computer. At each stage of analysis, special fluorescent molecules become attached to the genetic material under analysis, and a laser illuminates them while a high-resolution digital camera takes detailed pictures. The computer analyzes these digital pictures to create a map that shows the sequence of codes in the gene. If you can imagine seeing your city at night from an airplane and recognizing the shapes of the streets in your neighborhood just by looking at the winking patterns of streetlights, then you have the general idea. By comparing the sequences from healthy and diseased tissue, or among different individuals within a species, or between different generations of the same organism, scientists can develop an understanding of why and how creatures evolve, behave, and adapt as they do.

The shape of DNA (the molecule of genetic information that encodes every characteristic of every organism) was not even understood until 1953, when James Watson and Francis Crick used X-ray images collected by Rosalind Franklin to uncover its double helix structure. Twenty more years passed before scientists could even sequence the genes of a single organism, a virus so simple and tiny that you would have to line up more than 2,500 of them in a row to reach the width of a human hair (Fiers et al., 1976). Another 20 years passed, and computers became more ubiquitous, cheaper, and smaller, all of which permitted the development of automation that made rapid gene sequencing possible. In 2003, scientists released an initial database containing many of the more than 3 billion *base-pairs* (the most basic codes contained in DNA) in the human genome. Government funding from the U.S., Japan, China, Germany, and France to support this project topped $3 billion, and the effort spanned 13 years. However, that period was also one of rapid growth and development in information technology such that the gene sequencing of a complete human genome can now be accomplished in a matter of weeks for a few thousand dollars. In 1990, it cost about $10 to sequence each base-pair in a genetic sample. Continual advances in the underlying technology will soon make the price less than 1 cent per base-pair (Kurzweil, 2005). If you bought a copy of this book, within a few years, the same amount of money will probably suffice to analyze, in detail, hundreds of key sequences in your own genetic structure that could illuminate your future prospects for cancer, heart disease, and hundreds of other diseases. Although the chemistry and biology involved in gene sequencing are centrally and critically important, the factors that decreased the price of sequencing and increased the speed of sequencing were incredibly rapid advancements in information technology. These were reductions in the costs of the information technology and increases in its speed and other capabilities that outstrip all other historical advancements in human technologies.

Scientists sometimes call gene sequencing and related data-intensive activities *bioinformatics*. Bioinformatics refers to the use of information technology along with molecular biology to detect, catalog, store, and analyze the characteristics of the building blocks of life. In the span of one generation of scientists—from the past of Roger Arliner Young to the present of Agnes A. Day—bioinformatics has profoundly altered and accelerated the science of biology. Nearly every scientist has a computer on his or her desk—although it's probably used for email more than anything else—but behind the scenes, in the laboratory, the computers that run the experiments, record the results, perform the calculations, and display the findings make it possible for one biology graduate student to accomplish in a week about the same amount of scientific work that it took Roger Arliner Young a lifetime to do.

This word *informatics* keeps popping up all over the place. In addition to bioinformatics, we have medical informatics, health informatics, chemical informatics, business informatics, and social informatics. The word became popular in Great Britain before it migrated to the U.S., but now we use the word rather loosely to refer to a combination of technology, information science, computer science, and information management. This vague mixture of terms and fields reflects both the complexity and the newness of the information professions. The development of a piece of machinery as complex as a gene sequencer requires many different experts with a wide range of knowledge areas: microprocessor architecture, software, databases, information retrieval, statistical analysis, networking, sensors, and image processing (and this list doesn't mention all of the chemists and biologists involved). What many of these experts have in common is a concern for the creation, manipulation, analysis, storage, and retrieval of information. In this book, we refer to them collectively as information professionals. Information professionals provide the "informatics" that fuel areas such as bioinformatics and business informatics.

As the gene sequencing example shows, informatics makes rapid advances possible in fields that developed long before computers were invented. In business, information technology and algorithms make it possible for your credit card company to discover fraudulent use of your account at the moment it happens. In chemistry, automated experimental platforms make it possible to screen rapidly thousands of variations on compounds that might be the next breakthrough in cancer treatment. In law offices, computerized search and retrieval of case law takes the place of the painstaking use of massive libraries of legal books that were outdated almost as soon as they were printed. In healthcare, databases of medical records make it possible to detect emerging strains of influenza and other communicable diseases before they erupt into epidemics. In short, the use of information and technology is creating revolutions in nearly every human endeavor. For every doctor, lawyer, executive, scientist, and bureaucrat who is at work today, we have a number of information professionals who imagine, develop, and create the information superstructure that makes all of those other professions what they are. For every profession that exists tomorrow, we will need even more of those information architects because growth, advancement, innovation, and entrepreneurship in business, science, education, and government will become ever more entwined and dependent upon information and the information technology that hosts it. Information professionals will continue to increase their influence on the productivity and advancement of almost every other profession, and the demand for trained information professionals will continue to grow as a result. But what will these information jobs look like? Will they be the same as current jobs? Will these jobs be outsourced from the U.S. to other countries? In the next few chapters, we will examine and try to answer these questions.

References

Day, A. A., McQuillan, C. I., Termine, J. D., & Young, M. R. (1987). Molecular cloning and sequence analysis of the cDNA for small proteoglycan II of bovine bone. *Biochemical Journal, 248*(3), 801.

Fiers, W., Contreras, R., Duerinck, F., Haegeman, G., Iserentant, D., Merregaert, J., et al. (1976). Complete nucleotide sequence of bacteriophage MS2 RNA: Primary and secondary structure of the replicase gene. *Nature, 260*(5551), 500–507.

Kurzweil, R. (2005). *The singularity is near: When humans transcend biology.* New York: Viking.

Manning, K. (1989). Roger Arliner Young, scientist. *Sage: A Scholarly Journal on Black Women, 6*(2), 3–7.

Sullivan, O. R. (2002). *Black stars: African American scientists and inventors.* New York: John Wiley and Sons.

CHAPTER 4

Horseshoes to Biofuels: Why Technology Development Gets Easier All the Time

*I have never been lost, but I will admit to being
confused for several weeks.*
                    —Daniel Boone, American pioneer

Most people think of Daniel Boone as a legendary colonial-era adventurer best known for his explorations of Kentucky, but before that, Boone was a blacksmith from a family of blacksmiths (Morgan, 2007, p. 436). In the 1700s and 1800s, blacksmithing was partly science and partly art: The essential principles of metallurgy had been known for thousands of years, but the chemical basis of the mixtures and transformations that could make metal flexible, brittle, malleable, springy, or corrosion-resistant were just beginning to be understood in the 18th century. Blacksmiths such as Boone understood some of these principles without any formal knowledge of the chemistry or physics involved. Among his many other talents and activities, Boone shod horses for George Washington's army. Each iron horseshoe was cast into its basic shape in a mass-manufacturing process but fitted to each particular horse and hoof in a customization activity that was a craft learned and refined over a period of many years. In that era, most metalworking (e.g., the building of iron bridges) was accomplished in the same way: a primitive mass production of simple component parts followed by customizations created by artisans who possessed mastery of their art through apprenticeship and experience.

In the intervening 200 years since Boone's lifetime, metallurgy has mostly shifted away from art and toward science. As the atomic nature of matter has emerged into common knowledge, chemists and physicists have obtained a comprehensive understanding of the processes by which metals and alloys gain their properties. Advances in manufacturing have led to ready-to-use, precision, modular metal components that can be assembled on site. The artisan metalworker still exists—M. Smyth Boone, a descendant of Daniel Boone, creates artistic decorations and household hardware using a forge that would have been recognizable to his legendary forefather—but for the most part, the contemporary creation of metal parts is subsidiary to the larger task of creating complex systems with metal components.

For example, consider Piedmont Biofuels, based in North Carolina. This firm creates small biodiesel reactors that change organic waste oils, such as the cooking oil from making french fries, into a fuel that diesel motors can burn quite efficiently and arguably with fewer environmental problems than petroleum products. On its website (www.biofuels.coop), Piedmont shows a basic parts list for its biodiesel reactor that comprises 24 mostly metal items that anyone can purchase from an appropriate parts supplier. Of course, some of the parts, such as the small electric pump, are themselves composed of hundreds of discrete metallic and nonmetallic parts. Counting every individual metal component in each of the parts described, the reactor probably consists of no more than about 500 individual pieces, including all of the screws, washers, rivets, and so forth. For instance, the electric pump contains several ball bearings, each containing up to a dozen individual steel balls, each of which was mass manufactured to a tolerance of 2/10,000ths or 3/10,000ths of an inch (about 5/1,000ths of a millimeter).

Fortunately, the employees at Piedmont Biofuels did not need to give the slightest thought to the manufacture of ball bearings. Their work focused almost exclusively on creating a complex chemical transformation system—the biodiesel reactor—from basic, off-the-shelf, modular metal components readily available from a variety of suppliers and manufacturers. This example illustrates how straightforward it is to become a "power user" of an underlying technology (e.g., the complex metallurgy that produces reliable ball bearings), without any knowledge of or special talent with how that technology was itself created. The Piedmont employees are experts in the manufacture of biodiesel and have created a complex system in their area of expertise without much knowledge or concern for the various component technologies.

The same transformation—paralleling the change from horseshoes to biofuels—has occurred in the world of information, only 10 times faster than in the world of metalworking (about 50 years instead of 500). Before the 1950s, the creation and manipulation of information was as much craft as it was science, although many important underlying principles, particularly in mathematics, had been known for hundreds of years. The most important medium of information storage and transmission up until the 20th century was arguably the printed word. Mass production of books, like the mass production of horseshoes, had been around for years, but it used to be quite a labor-intensive process that required a variety of artisans and many expensive resources to produce a quality result (Eisenstein, 1979). As an interesting side note, printing and metallurgy were blood brothers throughout the 19th century because of so-called hot metal typesetting, a process of injecting molten lead into a mold that contained concave shapes of letters and numbers: The resulting frame contained a line of type that could be inked and stamped repeatedly onto paper. But once it was printed, a book was difficult to modify because each page was a fixed composition of type with the spaces, letters, and numbers organized immovably into their respective lines of text. Indexing, illustrating, printing, cutting, binding, and finishing a book required seasoned experts who had mastered their crafts through extensive experience. Hot metal typesetters were in some ways the Daniel Boones of the precomputerized world of information.

The rapid development of the transistor in the 1950s and integrated circuits in the 1960s revolutionized the production, transmission, and storage of information first by making digital computers practical and later by making them vanishingly inexpensive (Brinkman, Haggan, & Troutman, 1997). Over the course of a little more than a half century, information management has moved from the horseshoe era to the biofuels era. In 1954, using a computer required mastering an arcane language called Fortran (which stood for "formula translation"), the first of the so-called high-level programming languages (Wexelblat, 1981). A person needed a solid understanding of mathematics to use Fortran, and the purposes for which Fortran was used themselves were quite mathematical (e.g., calculating missile trajectories). Playing a game, writing a novel, or keeping a calendar by using Fortran to program the computer would have been quite difficult, primitive, and time-consuming since the only input came from a typewriter, and there was no screen to display what you were doing.

However, it only took about 10 years to get to the point that you could see what you were doing on a screen and could point at something on the screen using a mouse. Another 5 years and we had the precursor to the modern internet called the ARPANET, and suddenly, it was possible to send information from one person to another via a networked computer.

In 1971, Ray Tomlinson, then an employee of the Boston-based Bolt, Beranek and Newman company, sent the first email message between two computers (Howard & Jones, 2004). Unlike Alexander Graham Bell, who made that legendary first ever phone call to his assistant Mr. Watson, Tomlinson has since forgotten what that first email message said.

Personal computers began to arrive on the consumer market in 1974, and the first spreadsheet and word processing programs arrived about 5 years later. Just as with the Piedmont Biofuels example, the workings of the individual components in these devices had started to become irrelevant to the process of creating a complex system. Using the first commercially viable spreadsheet program,

VisiCalc, a person could create a financial model of a business—fixed costs, variable expenses, revenue projections, return on investment, and so forth—with no understanding whatsoever of the many transistors humming away inside the aged ancestor of today's iPhones, the Apple II personal computer.

Fast forward to the present, and we find that home computer users can set up their own wireless home network with minimal understanding of radio frequency emissions, data packets, or programming. Certainly, setting up such a network with appropriate security or attaching devices to the network, such as network storage, does require some knowledge of the underlying technology. Extending the example further, setting up a wireless network for a large company—perhaps one that has 1,000 employees across several floors of a large building—requires a quite sophisticated understanding of the various devices and their limitations. However, what it does not require is the ability to construct an integrated circuit from scratch or code an embedded operating system for a network routing device. This situation exactly parallels the transition from horseshoes to biofuels: A person with domain expertise (biofuels or networking) can construct an enormously complex system (a biodiesel reactor or a large wireless network) from separate elements (e.g., a pump or a wireless access point) without knowing everything about how each element was itself constructed.

Two key ideas make this possible: modularity and connectivity. Modularity hides the complexity of an underlying system in a package that a person can use without knowing exactly how it was made or how it works. You probably don't know how to create a transistor or a ball bearing (and neither do we), but you can use these elements effectively nonetheless. Connectivity makes possible the combining of smaller, simpler subsystems to create substantially larger, more complex systems. In the biofuels example, we had various valves, pipes, and spigots, all of which were engineered to have appropriate dimensions and shapes so that they could be connected. In the wireless networking example, we have various devices that use common and nearly universal jacks and cables to connect, along with agreed upon languages (or protocols, as engineers call them) to communicate with each other.

Over time, modularity and connectivity put more powerful capabilities—more system complexity—within the reach of a larger number of people. As each new generation of technological advancement encapsulates previous innovations in a modular, interconnectable shell, the resulting capabilities offered by the technology expand exponentially. The most popular computer operating system in the world, Microsoft Windows, required millions of person hours and nearly 10 calendar years of development before it was ready for practical use (i.e., from the introduction of MS-DOS in 1981 to the release of Windows 3.0 in 1990). Engineers at Microsoft had to do everything from scratch—they had very little that they could reuse from previous projects and many new, untried capabilities to develop. In the early 1990s, Mosaic, which was the first practical browser for the internet, took a few people (mainly Marc Andreessen and Eric Bina) a couple of years to write. These developers had a substantial set of previously developed capabilities to build upon. The first version of Facebook, the popular social networking application, was created by Mark Zuckerberg in a month or two (late 2003 and early 2004). Zuckerberg had the advantage of drawing upon an advanced base of existing tools and infrastructure. Consider the following tiny chunk of the common webpage building language known as html:

```
<object width="425" height="344">
 <embed
 src="http://www.youtube.com/v/GHDo8ki
 Ws1k" type="application/x-shockwave-
 flash" width="425" height="344">
 </embed>
</object>
```

This somewhat inscrutable but very compact set of instructions allows users who can create a simple webpage to include a full-color, full-motion video of a musical performance with no other programming, software, or equipment needed. This novel capability is possible because the engineers at YouTube have built an extensive and modular infrastructure to which anyone in the world can connect at no charge and with very little expertise.

While Microsoft Windows, Mosaic, Facebook, and YouTube vary widely in complexity and scope, each has arguably had a powerful impact on our society and culture, the way we work and play, and the way we look at the world. As technological achievements, each of these examples has something special about it, but the most striking point is how much simpler it became in each succeeding case to create a new information technology wonder. The information field, like no other historical area of human accomplishment, has accelerated the capabilities of information creators and users from the Daniel Boone stage to the Piedmont Biofuels stage within the span of less than one lifetime.

Nowhere has this trend manifested itself more strongly than in the open source software movement. In 1991, a young Finnish man named Linus Torvalds had a crazy idea (Moon & Sproull, 2002). Torvalds appreciated the many useful features of a computer operating system called UNIX. This operating system, which had animated the activities of many types of computers for more than two decades, was powerful, flexible, and expandable—or it had been expandable until a private company got hold of it and began charging lots of money for people to use it (Bretthauer, 2002). Torvalds decided that he would create his own operating system that would replicate many of the capabilities of Unix but that also would not remain under the exclusive control of a single company. Torvalds created the "kernel" of the operating system, which contains the central control functions that choose among the various tasks the computer should do and how long it should do each one. He then realized that the job was bigger than he thought and that he needed help with building all of the other important parts of the system. At this point, he did something very unusual: He gave away all of the work that he had done. He simply published every single line of computer code that he had created for the project. Soon afterwards, another amazing thing occurred. Other people volunteered to help him. They donated their time and expertise to create a totally open, totally free operating system that anyone could use and modify. This operating system bears the name Linux.[1]

By most measures, Linux was and is still considered to be an enormous success. It is installed on millions of computers worldwide, and it has an active community of volunteer supporters who fix old problems and help to develop new features. Linux is complex and has many interacting pieces and parts, but it is nonetheless quite reliable and error-free, thanks to the efforts of these many volunteers. It is also remarkably secure: The operating system prevents unauthorized access to information, makes sure that information stored in it remains accurate, and consistently provides requested information to authorized users in a timely way—the three fundamental aspects of computer security that engineers like to promote. Linux has provided commercial success to a number of companies, such as Red Hat, that make a living out of helping users manage the installation, servicing, and updating of the operating system. Perhaps most important, Linux spawned an entirely new way of creating software using small armies of volunteers to create a product that eventually becomes publicly released and free for all to use.

Individuals who volunteer their time and effort to open source projects have a variety of motivations for doing so. Commonly, an individual has a hobbyist's interest in an area such as digital photography and is dissatisfied with the cost or capabilities of available commercial software tools. This person might become involved in an open source project to create photo-editing software. Other individuals may have an interest in honing their skills as software creators, so they volunteer for an open source project that will allow them to practice a certain programming language. More recently, employees of certain technology companies (e.g., IBM) receive work assignments from their firms instructing them to spend time assisting in the development of open source software systems. Some companies, such as Sun Microsystems, have even developed their own open source software systems as a conscious business strategy. One of the best known projects from Sun is the OpenOffice productivity tools suite (www.openoffice.org), which contains a word processor and spreadsheet that users can download, install, use, and modify freely.

The OpenOffice example shows that some businesses have discovered ways of making money from a product that is given away freely. Partly as a result of this, the number of open source software projects has exploded over recent years. Two of the websites that serve as clearinghouses for open source software are SourceForge (source forge.net) and freshmeat (freshmeat.net). Text posted on the SourceForge website (apps.sourceforge.net/trac/sourceforge/wiki/What%20is%20SourceForge.net?) says, "As of February, 2009, more than 230,000 software projects have been registered to use our services by more than 2 million registered users, making SourceForge.net the largest collection of open source tools and applications on the net." Nearly a quarter of a million open source software projects, millions of software developers (the registered users referred to in the quotation are mainly developers), and more millions of individuals who make frequent use of the open source software together comprise a worldwide community that leverages the power of technology in a radical new way.

The open source movement represents the tip of a technology democratization trend that puts more and more creative power in the hands of nonexperts. Many of those nearly quarter million open source software projects function in similar ways to building blocks, or the individual parts of the Piedmont biodiesel reactor. Individuals who are not actually expert programmers can nonetheless combine various software pieces and parts to make even more powerful technologies. In the 1950s, the Daniel Boone days of software development, a person essentially had to have a degree in computer science or computer engineering and years of experience to effectively accomplish the highly technical tasks of the day. Now, nearly anyone who is willing to take the time and make the effort to understand the functions of individual (modular) components of technology and the ways in which those modular components can be connected and combined can create a new technological capability.

This trend toward the democratization of technology suggests that a combination of *domain expertise*—an understanding of biology, chemistry, physics, art, music, history, psychology, or business— together with essential information and technology literacy provides the most powerful mix of skills that a worker can bring to the workplace. Although we will always need and will always have a few individuals who have extensive expertise in the fundamental underlying technologies—someone has to keep improving both ball bearings and integrated circuits—the vast majority of people who take advantage of information technology to solve problems in society will not be engineers or scientists themselves in the classic way that we understand these professions. In the next chapter, we delve more deeply into this area by examining offshoring and outsourcing, two trends in information technology employment that have scared off many students from pursuing an interest in the information fields. Neither horseshoes nor ball bearings are commonly mass produced in the U.S. anymore: These manufacturing tasks have moved to places where labor is less expensive. The same is true of many basic forms of information technology. Nonetheless, there is an enormous pool of excellent jobs in the U.S. that involve the extensive use of information technologies to serve many important purposes in business, government, the military, and other areas. For reasons that we will examine next, some or many of these jobs are and will probably remain resistant to outsourcing.

Endnotes

1. Note that Richard Stallman, arguably the author of the first open source program, a text editing program called emacs, created many other elements of a UNIX-like operating system, which he called GNU. The Linux kernel, developed by Torvalds, together with the many elements of GNU comprised the original version of the operating system we now call Linux (Bretthauer, 2002).

References

Bretthauer, D. (2002). Open source software: A history. *Information Technology and Libraries, 21*(1), 3–11.

Brinkman, W. F., Haggan, D. E., & Troutman, W. W. (1997). A history of the invention of the transistor and where it will lead us. *IEEE Journal of Solid-State Circuits, 32*(12), 1858–1865.

Eisenstein, E. L. (1979). *The printing press as an agent of change: Communications and cultural transformations in early modern Europe.* Cambridge, U.K.: Cambridge University Press.

Howard, P. N., & Jones, S. (2004). *Society online: The Internet in context.* Thousand Oaks, CA: Sage.

Moon, J. Y., & Sproull, L. (2002). Essence of distributed work: The case of the Linux kernel. In P. J. Hinds & S. Kiesler (Eds.), *Distributed Work* (pp. 381–404). Cambridge, MA: MIT Press.

Morgan, R. (2007). *Boone: A Biography.* New York: Shannon Ravenel.

Wexelblat, R. L. (1981). *History of programming languages.* New York: Academic Press.

CHAPTER 5

Where's My Job?
How Outsourcing and
Offshoring Change Industries

India, with a population of 1.1 billion, and a middle class that is larger than the entire population of the U.S., is one of the world's largest untapped markets.
—Satveer Chaudhary (D), Minnesota State Senator

One branch of the first author's family hails from Brockton, Massachusetts, a city of fewer than 100,000 citizens in the southeastern part of the Bay State. Starting in the early 1800s and through to the 1930s, Brockton was the world powerhouse in shoe manufacturing (Porrazzo, 2007, pp. 2–4). At the peak of the "Shoe City's" dominance right around 1907, more than 15,000 workers held jobs in 431 different shoe and shoe-related manufacturing companies in and around the city. Brockton rose to its leadership position through a lucky combination of innovative ideas and mechanization. Industrial engineers from the local area developed machines that created and assembled the component parts of a shoe hundreds of times faster than shoemakers elsewhere in the world. More than 200 patents for new methods of shoe manufacturing emerged from area firms. Brockton factories were the first to mass produce shoe components that had distinctive shapes for left and right shoes. Prior to that, most mass-produced shoes had a generic shape, and people had a painful time breaking in each shoe to the proper shape for each foot. Entrepreneur Micah Faxon became Brockton's first millionaire from the revenues generated by his shoe factory, and in the 1800s, $1 million was a huge amount of money (in comparison, the U.S. purchase of all of Alaska and the Aleutian Islands in 1867 from Russia cost $7 million).

However, between 1930 and 1980, Brockton's shoe industry began a fitful decline. First, the stock market crash of 1929 and the subsequent worldwide economic depression softened the market for Brockton's shoes and created labor unrest as more and more people lost their jobs across Massachusetts and elsewhere in the U.S. Then, World War II changed the face of global markets, closing some, opening others, and leading to a variety of new sources of low-cost labor in the post-war period. In 1964, only 10 factories in Brockton remained in business. By the 1970s, just a handful of companies remained. Today, there is only one shoe manufacturer, which produces specialty shoes for golfers. A couple of other companies make specialized elements for shoes that are assembled elsewhere. According to City-Data.com,[1] Brockton's main employers are now in healthcare, waste management, and accommodation and food services, with an assortment of smaller firms that perform services or are involved in light manufacturing.

Journalist Jean Porrazzo (2007) quotes a local industrialist of the early 1900s as saying, "The Brockton shoe is today, as it always has been, the acknowledged and unquestioned leader in its class. The position of prominence should—must—be held. It can be maintained." Given this level of determination and commitment, how can Brockton's shoe industry have fallen so far? Where did all of the shoe factories go, and where are all of the jobs associated with those factories? Why were local, state, and federal governments powerless to stop the decline of the shoe manufacturing industry in the U.S.? We picked this example intentionally because we know that many readers already know the answers to some of these questions. The largest footwear companies in the world, such as Nike and Reebok, are U.S.-based multinational firms, and they supply millions of pairs of shoes every year to wholesalers and in turn to retail outlets around the world. Nike's world headquarters are in Beaverton, Oregon, while Reebok's headquarters are in Canton, Massachusetts, just a 20-minute drive from Brockton. The headquarters of these and other U.S. shoe firms are home to hundreds of managers and professionals, and the collective expertise of these individuals generates billions of dollars in annual revenue. However, if you pull off the shoe you are wearing at this moment, it is likely that the label indicates that it was not manufactured in the U.S. Your shoes might have been made in China or India or Vietnam or possibly somewhere in Central America. The reason your shoes are likely to have been made in that country is straightforward: The cost of paying workers in that country is considerably less than the cost of paying U.S. workers. Because of mechanization, many of the jobs involved in shoe manufacturing require relatively low levels of skill and minimal training and education. Neither the wages nor the standard of living for many of those workers is anywhere near the average level in the U.S. You may see this situation as exploitation, or you may see it as an unavoidable manifestation of capitalism. But either way, if your shoes had been created by U.S. workers, they probably would have cost much more than you paid for them and very likely more than you would have wanted to pay.

But this is a book about information and technology, not shoes. The information industries, including technology manufacturing and software development, have undergone only the first few changes that occurred over the past century in the shoe industry, but the parallels are uncanny and the lessons valuable. From the period following World War II until the 1970s and 1980s, the U.S. was the undisputed world leader in information technology, software development, telecommunications, electronics manufacturing, and most of the other areas of the information industries. U.S. researchers created the first workable digital electronic computer, the transistor, the integrated circuit, and all of the high-level software programming languages available at the time. The first academic computer science program ever established was at Purdue University in 1962 (Rice &

Rosen, 2004). The first PhD in computer science was awarded by The Pennsylvania State University in 1965. At one point, the U.S. had more schools of library and information science than the rest of the world combined (Ostler, Dahlin, & Willardson, 1995). The U.S.-based firm IBM invented the personal computer; the operating system for that computer, MS-DOS, was put into place by a young U.S. entrepreneur and software developer named William H. Gates III, better known now as the billionaire philanthropist Bill Gates. Most of the key technological developments leading up to the creation of the internet were accomplished in U.S. laboratories and universities (Rosenzweig, 1998). If Brockton was the "Shoe City" of the 19th century, then the U.S. was the "Information Country" of the 20th.

Much as the Brockton shoe industry began its inexorable transformation during the Great Depression and World War II, the U.S. information industry began its gradual shift during the Korean War and the steep wage inflation period in the U.S. during the 1960s and early 1970s. During the Korean War, Japan changed its monetary policies in a way that encouraged the development of monopolies, most notably in the television manufacturing industry (Schwartzman, 1993, pp. 12–14). The powerful Japanese governmental agency, the Ministry of International Trade and Industry, made it possible for Sony, Hitachi, Toshiba, and other Japanese firms to price Japanese-made televisions so that they were quite attractive for U.S. consumers to purchase and noticeably cheaper than the brands made by U.S. manufacturers. Meanwhile, during the late 1960s and early 1970s, economic conditions in the U.S. caused workers' wages to increase rapidly, with the result that goods such as televisions that were manufactured in the U.S. cost more to make and as a result had to be priced higher. In a book about the Japanese television industry, David Schwartzman (1993, p. 14) reported that when the average manufacturing wage in the U.S. was $3.23 per hour in 1966, the corresponding figure in Japan was 51 cents. U.S. television manufacturers dropped like bricks, and much of the industrial support structure—manufacturing of the component electronics, circuit boards, picture tubes, and so forth—went with it.

In 1985, the final cut occurred: The giant multinational conglomerate General Electric purchased an ailing RCA, Radio Corporation of America. For more than 65 years, RCA was a shining gem of U.S. high-technology dominance, and then it was sliced into small pieces and sold off or given away (Abramson, 2003, p. 112). General Electric *donated* RCA's research labs, essentially as a tax write-off, to Stanford University. General Electric closed the remainder of RCA's U.S. operations related to electronics design and manufacturing or moved them overseas. The television, arguably the most common and widely used high-technology information distribution device in history, was no longer a U.S. product. Go over to your local Walmart today and look at the manufacturing labels on the HDTVs, and you will almost certainly not see a label with the words, "Proudly Made in the USA."

As the television manufacturing industry dissolved, so did many other electronic component and device manufacturers. As countries such as Japan, Korea, Taiwan, and Singapore ramped up their technological capabilities and while their labor costs remained low, they experienced a manufacturing boom that propelled them upwards among the world economies. Interestingly, Japan's wages are now the highest in the world, and manufacturing of televisions, as well as other labor-intensive devices, has migrated to other countries such as China and Vietnam where the wages are considerably lower (Ashenfelter & Jurajda, 2004).

A related trend that many find extremely disturbing is the migration of software development jobs to countries with lower wages. For several decades between the 1950s and the 1980s, U.S. universities and research labs promoted the idea that software development was an art and a science that required extensive training, at least a bachelor's degree, and years of experience. The idea holds a certain amount of truth: The earliest large computers, inscrutable installations with lights flashing and tapes spinning, were indeed quite complex to master. Early programming languages such as Fortran, PL/1, and Lisp had many arcane aspects and few of the labor saving features of modern software development environments. The absence of graphical interfaces and the use of unwieldy storage media such as paper tape and punch cards made computers seem complex and mysterious. But it was a mistake to assume that these barriers would persist forever, and as Chapter 4 discussed, the tasks of technology development generally and software development in particular have become friendlier and more powerful over time. Any literate person who possesses a passing familiarity with computers can now learn how to create a simple script in a few hours. Becoming a *coder* (someone who creates the most essential instructions for computer applications) can occur in a semester or two of intensive study. Full-fledged software engineers, with knowledge of a range of project coordination tools, languages, software development kits, and application environments, need only study for a couple of years to obtain a basic level of competency.

In the 1980s, some very bright people in India recognized this idea and decided that people in their country, which contains the second-largest number of English-speaking citizens in the world, might come to dominate parts of the software industry, given the right training and opportunities (Athreye, 2005). An official government policy document concerning promotion of educational opportunities in computer science and software engineering was approved in 1986. Subsequently, the number of qualified software workers in India began to explode, and Indian firms became known on the world stage as the premier low-cost providers of custom software applications, as opposed to shrink-wrapped, commercially packaged software such as Microsoft Word (Bhatnagar & Madon, 1997). U.S. and European businesses in all industries soon learned that an outside service firm could design and build large software projects at a much lower price than their own employees could. As a result, many firms began to outsource or offshore their software development activities. As this movement occurred, the companies also fired their own employees who had been doing the jobs that were now outsourced. This was pretty horrible for the U.S. employees who were fired, but anyone who owned stock in the company was glad to see such cost-cutting initiatives and bigger profits.

The distinction between outsourcing and offshoring is an important one. Outsourcing simply means that a company decides to hire another company to do a job. For example, when a bank needs a new building, it hires a construction company to do the work. This is outsourcing at its simplest, and it makes sense to everyone: You don't want your bank manager designing roofs or foundations. The bank may also hire outside firms to perform janitorial services, security, transportation services, background checking, and an entire host of other activities that are not part of the core function of a bank. All of these comprise examples of outsourcing, and arguably none of them is a problem for the economic viability of the bank or the community where the bank resides or the country in which the bank does business. In fact, this situation seems healthy in that new businesses spring up in the community to provide needed expertise and services.

In contrast, when a company offshores a function, such as manufacturing or engineering, it hires a firm in another country—often the one with the lowest wage rates—to perform the function. If the bank in our example needs a custom software application built, it might choose to hire a firm in India to do the job. This choice takes money out of the community and the country where the bank resides and puts it into the country where the offshore work is accomplished. This move arguably serves the best interests of the bank because it lowers the cost of acquiring an important technology tool that it needs. But some have argued that it hurts the bank's community and the country as a whole because it represents a lost opportunity for a worker in that community to do the job for the bank. Some people describe this scenario as "jobs lost to offshoring," and they suggest that this trend of moving jobs to where the labor is cheapest is new and dangerous, and that it must be stopped.

However, we know from the Brockton shoe example that offshoring is definitely not new. Professional economists spend lots of time arguing about whether offshoring is bad or good and how exactly it affects the economy of the region or country where it originates. Government leaders may listen to one of these economists in order to decide on regulations or to figure out how to appease their constituencies, particularly those who have recently lost their jobs.

But for most of us, arguments about the benefits or pitfalls of off-shoring are just noise: Any individual citizen is unlikely (in the short term anyway) to sway any of these companies from choosing to out-source or offshore. Instead, each person has to look out for his or her own employment interests, including understanding why companies offshore and how they do it, in order to anticipate these changes and avoid being badly affected by them. In the information industries, which by their nature often change very quickly, it is especially important to stay aware of employment trends because of the changes described in the previous chapter. A job that is difficult to do today, and which requires extensive education and experience, may become much simpler tomorrow as the technology tools become more powerful and less expensive. As soon as that job becomes easy enough for a less-experienced or less-well-educated worker at another company to do, there is a possibility that a company will out-source the work. If a worker at that other company happens to be in a different country, especially where the cost or standard of living is lower, than that of the person who lost the job, then the outsourced job has become an offshored job. In Brockton, the shoe industry began to experience outsourcing and offshoring a century ago because the technology of mechanized manufacturing made the jobs in the shoe factories simpler and easier. As a result, the workers needed less training and experience. All over the U.S., the informa-tion technology industries, and most recently the software program-ming industry, began to experience outsourcing and offshoring two decades ago because the jobs became progressively easier *and* other countries realized the importance of those jobs. They also began a concentrated effort to educate their workforce to do the jobs.

At this point, you may be thinking that this sounds like a kind of jobs "arms race." A person goes to the effort of getting a college degree and has built up his or her knowledge and experience in order to be able to do a certain job well, just in time for that job to become routine enough that some other company in some other country can do it cheaper. Now you have to get more education and experience so that you can move into a new job that is so cutting-edge and innovative that it can't be outsourced, at least for now.

This scenario may seem daunting and depressing, or you may find it exciting and challenging, but it is likely to be an accurate picture of the future career path for many U.S. workers and not just in information technology. Many, if not most, U.S. jobs in manufacturing have been in this mode for a long time. Some jobs in the information field also seem particularly prone to these transformations because information is easy to move over long distances, but these changes are affecting virtually every area of human endeavor. In the healthcare field, it is now routine to transmit an X-ray or other diagnostic image to another country to be read, interpreted, and reported on by a radiologist who gets paid far less than his or her counterpart in the U.S. When an experimental drug is tested for safety and efficacy in a human population, the testing program often occurs with volunteer participants from countries other than the U.S. In the publishing industry, book companies often transmit their manuscripts overseas for copy editing, layout, and other tasks that used to be accomplished by U.S. workers. We all know about offshoring of customer service activities because each of us has spoken on the phone to a representative who is located in another country. Many of these customer service representatives receive extensive training in order to emulate U.S. accents and to stay aware of trends in U.S. weather, news, and sports in order to provide callers with a "familiar" experience (Youngdahl & Ramaswamy, 2008). If you have been through the drive-through lane at a fast food restaurant lately, you may have noticed that the voice of the person who takes your order and the voice of the person at the window don't match. That may be because the restaurant has outsourced order-taking to a remote location (not necessarily in another country) where it can be done more efficiently, more accurately, or more cheaply.

In thinking about this situation, we can consider three kinds of work/jobs that are unlikely to be outsourced. The first type comprises service jobs that require *physical presence* of the worker at the location where the service is dispensed. Until robots get a whole lot better than they are today, when you go out to eat at a restaurant, you will be served by a human waiter or waitress, and your plates will be cleared by a human busser. When you need physical therapy, therapeutic massage, or chiropractic services, you must visit the office of a professional who puts "hands on" in the most literal sense of the term. When the water pump in your car fails, you will not have the option of shipping your vehicle to China to have it repaired.

The second type of outsource-resistant job is artisanal. When you go to a craft fair to watch the glass artist create a transparent masterpiece and you purchase that unique sculpture for your living room, you are supporting a profession that has been around for hundreds of years and will persist indefinitely into the future, albeit on a small scale. If you are a dedicated guitarist and you decide to have an instrument custom made from exotic wood, you will probably engage a luthier from Vermont and not one from China (Brookes, 2006). Likewise, if you enjoy ballet, opera, or concerts, you will travel to a nearby venue to see your favorite performer in action. Although some people don't mind watching a videotaped performance of their favorite performers, many people get a unique level of enjoyment from seeing live performances. This translates into non-"outsourceable" work for the performers. In artisanal work, each worker (whether artist, sculptor, musician, dancer, or something else) makes a unique creation or experience that meets the following two criteria: 1) It does not scale up to a level where hundreds or thousands of people in another country can do the same work economically, and/or 2) The consumer of the product or service wants to have some personal involvement in its design, creation, or performance.

The third and final outsource-resistant job category, and the one that is the essential focus of this book, is the innovative job with an entrepreneurial focus that gains its uniqueness from a combination of up-to-date knowledge and the imaginative application of that knowledge to an important problem that no one has solved before. Such jobs are difficult to outsource because no one has (yet) figured out a way to educate large numbers of people for the novel combination of skills and creativity. Various pundits have coined names such as *info-vator* or *infopreneur* for the people who do this kind of work. Alternatively, we prefer the more prosaic term *information profes-sional*. Whatever label we use, the job has some key features that set it apart from other jobs that are more likely to be outsourced or off-shored.

The job involves working on difficult or intractable problems that cannot be solved (at least in the present) either by automation or by using cheap labor to perform repetitive tasks. One example of such a job is an information security analyst. Despite the availability of hundreds of different information security software and hardware products, the human ability to understand the nature of a cyberattack on a computer system remains unrivaled. Professionals who hold jobs such as this one use information tools in combinations and strategies that nobody has tried before. These jobs also incorporate aspects of the two other job categories, the service worker and the artisan, by providing a human touch on projects that cannot be replicated by an individual who is hundreds or thousands of miles away. Many jobs in the information professions require first-hand, face-to-face interaction with end users of information systems in order to understand at a deep, intuitive level how the users think about the problems they are trying to solve with an information system.

To successfully obtain and keep a job of this nature requires a unique mixture of capabilities. An information professional must have an essential level of working knowledge across all of the fundamental information technology areas: networks, databases, internet technologies (e.g., web programming), operating systems, and basic architectural models (e.g., client-server and peer-to-peer). By *working knowledge*, we mean having a general understanding of how it works and not deep expertise in each area. Likewise, the information professional has to be a bit of a social scientist with a working knowledge of psychology, sociology, and anthropology: knowing how people work individually and in groups, understanding how people choose and use their technology tools, and anticipating when people will resist or embrace change. One offshoot of this "social scientist" mind-set is that it is also highly valuable to be able to communicate and interact effectively with a diverse range of other people. Finally, the information professional needs an area of depth, or one specific domain in which he or she has an extra level of knowledge and skill that few others possess. Carrying our example forward from the previous paragraph, an information security professional who also has a legal background has an incredible advantage in the job market and the workplace. Some researchers have referred to this mixture of broad knowledge and one (or more) areas of close expertise as a "T-shaped" structure (Hansen & Von Oetinger, 2001). These "T-shaped" professionals combine general knowledge that allows them to communicate with experts in a variety of areas together with their own area of expertise.

The "T-shaped" information professional adds unique value to a business, in a way that is difficult to replicate and in situations that require being physically present on the scene. Cutting-edge technical knowledge maintained through continuing, lifelong education, combined with the social scientist's knack for examining and understanding how information users solve problems, allows information professionals to constantly reinvent and revitalize their job roles as new challenges emerge. This is hard to outsource, and it requires a creative, interdisciplinary approach to a person's educational experiences. In the next section of the book, we paint a portrait of the wide range of job activities that these information professionals do. We'll hear perspectives on the information professional's role from students and working professionals. And we will see how each one met the challenges of developing these unique mixtures of technology and people skills.

Endnotes

1. www.city-data.com/zips/02301.html (accessed June 7, 2009).

References

Abramson, A. (2003). *The history of television, 1942 to 2000.* Jefferson, NC: McFarland & Company.

Ashenfelter, O., & Jurajda, S. (2004). *Cross-country comparisons of wage rates: The McWage Index.* Princeton, NJ: Princeton University.

Athreye, S. S. (2005). The Indian software industry and its evolving service capability. *Industrial and Corporate Change, 14*(3), 393–418.

Bhatnagar, S. C., & Madon, S. (1997). The Indian software industry: Moving towards maturity. *Journal of Information Technology, 12*(4), 277–288.

Brookes, T. (2006). *Guitar: An American life.* New York: Grove Press.

Hansen, M. T., & Von Oetinger, B. (2001). Introducing T-shaped managers: Knowledge management's next generation. *Harvard Business Review, 79*(3), 106.

Ostler, L. J., Dahlin, T. C., & Willardson, J. D. (1995). *The closing of American library schools: Problems and opportunities.* Westport, CT: Greenwood Press.

Porrazzo, J. (2007, September 24, 2007). March of progress: The rise and decline of Shoe City, U.S.A. *The Brockton Enterprise.*

Rice, J. R., & Rosen, S. (2004). Computer sciences at Purdue University—1962 to 2000. *IEEE Annals of the History of Computing, 26*(2), 48–61.

Rosenzweig, R. (1998). Wizards, bureaucrats, warriors, and hackers: Writing the history of the Internet. *American Historical Review,* 1530–1552.

Schwartzman, D. (1993). *The Japanese television cartel: A study based on Matsushita v. Zenith.* Ann Arbor, MI: University of Michigan Press.

Youngdahl, W., & Ramaswamy, K. (2008). Offshoring knowledge and service work: A conceptual model and research agenda. *Journal of Operations Management, 26*(2), 212–221.

PART 2

What Information Professionals Do in School and at Work

This section of the book is designed to give an updated, realistic, and unbiased preview of the information professions, with special attention to some of the occupational culture issues that may influence students' decisions to join the information professions as well as current workers' choices to remain in the professions. Most of these chapters provide quotes from people we interviewed. Chapter 6 discusses what it is like to be an information professional in training. Chapter 7 discusses barriers that students encounter, particularly women and students of color, as they undertake education and pre-professional activities in the information field. Chapter 8 turns the focus to the current workplace context by describing what the current workplace is like for information professionals. Chapter 9 discusses barriers and challenges faced by current workers in the information professions. Chapter 10 ties together the rest of the chapters in this section with a report on our analysis of the occupational culture of information technology professionals.

CHAPTER 6

The Student Perspective on the Information Field

Basically, our goal is to organize the world's information and to make it universally accessible and useful. That's our mission.

—Larry Page, Google co-founder

College sophomore Cayla's[1] black hair is spiked into a 4 inch-high fin, peaking front to back over the top of her scalp. In a short-sleeved sienna shirt and a polka-dotted white jumper, Cayla looks like a younger, punk version of fashion model Tyra Banks. It turns out that this impression is partly correct because, as our research team watched a digital video of Cayla's interview, she revealed the following:

> A lot of people who see me on campus think that by how I dress that and how I walk—I may have on something fashionable on or look glamorous—everyone thinks that I am a fashion major, which I am not. I am an information technology major … I know that by having that IT background I am not restricted to one mainstream industry. I can work anywhere, such as NBC; I can work in a fashion company because technology is implemented every day in industry, and it is increasing. So that is why I do it, and I know that I can help contribute to a fashion industry if I decided to do

that. But having the IT major is more stable than a fashion major.

We conducted interviews with dozens of current and former college students such as Cayla who were majoring or minoring in information and technology programs. We also ran a series of focus groups in which anywhere from six to 10 students would gather to talk about their experiences in high school and beyond. We found some surprising ideas and attitudes among them. Most notably, we found that our stereotypes about the experiences, interests, skills, and plans of these students were not always accurate. We also found that the students sometimes held myths about the information professions that were equally inaccurate.

To begin at the beginning, we asked a number of college freshmen how they got into the information field. Almost universally, students referred to some early experience with computers—in high school or before—and to the encouragement they received from a family member. For instance, freshman IT student Mary said:

> I would say my dad is the biggest influence. He started out as an engineer and went into the business world, so for management I would say he's my biggest influence for that. I've always been good at computers so that was always interesting to me. I like technology, and it's such a big part of life. I'm always able to fix my friends' computers and do all of that stuff so …

Another freshman, Rebecca, said something quite similar:

> My dad kind of motivated me because he's in this industry. He works at a pharmaceutical company so he used to always come home and talk about who is developing what and all this new technology, and he came up with some kind of program. That interested me.

An interesting aspect of Rebecca's comment is that her father worked as an information technologist in the pharmaceutical industry. As Chapter 3 discussed, due to the rise of genomics and bioinformatics, the pharmaceutical industry currently spends enormous amounts of money annually on IT professionals and infrastructure. Having a background in IT and biology provides a mix of skills that pharmaceutical companies value.

Another freshman student, Jana, commented on her work with computers in high school:

> Well, for me, in high school I just was really interested in computers all the time when we would have computers at our house, you know just everything. I just like to play around and just like download stuff, and then fix the computer and run the virus scan and everything because no one else in my family would do it. The computer would freeze, and they would just leave it there and no one would do anything. I just sort of took the initiative to figure out how to fix it, how to get rid of the viruses and things like that, and then it just grew from there. I just kept trying to learn, and that's why I am here.

Interestingly, if students did not have the opportunity to work with computers at home, they might not get the exposure in high school that would spark an interest in the field. Freshman student Mark made the following comments about the mistaken impressions and lack of knowledge of the information field that his peers had in high school:

> You go to high school, you learn basic math, science, English … But a lot of times people don't know that IT is out there. I've had to tell every single one of my friends what IT is. They all think you'll just be sitting in a cubicle all your life. I don't think everyone knows that there is this middle [ground] between being a manager and computer

science. I've never met anyone except people in the field who know what that is, that it's here. I don't think the word is really out there. If people hear "information studies" they might think book shelving, libraries. People don't typically associate information with computers. I just thought computers were computers. Information was looking stuff up on the internet, maybe on Google, or in a library.

Mark's suggestion that people don't "associate information with computers" is similar to saying that people don't associate bicycles with transportation, but there is an important kernel of truth in his comment. As we spoke with more and more students, we found that many students who were unfamiliar with the information field had an assumption that many of jobs having to do with computers had something to do with building the computer itself (or the software in the computer). This is similar to saying that if you are interested in bicycles, then by definition, the main thing you do is repair them. Instead, we know that for most people a bicycle represents a way of getting around. Likewise, the role of computers in the information field is to "get around" with information. Information is the most important thing; the computer is really just a vehicle to work with it. Relatively few people in the information industries make their living actually building or fixing computers. Most people in the information industries work with information, and they mainly use computers as a technological tool to accomplish this.

With that said, we found a wide degree of variation in how involved students wanted to be in the technological side of the information business. In the comments that follow, Dara, Yvonne, and Mary cover the spectrum in their opinions:

Dara: I'm more of a people person rather than [someone who prefers to] sit at a desk all day in front of a computer. I mean that's just not me, that's not what I want to do. But the fact that IT has a lot of base in management I think is really important, that everybody needs to be aware of organizational structures and how people work together and how technology relates to it. And then classes like [Operating Systems Administration], which is so technical and all, that's what turns me off. I'm like OK, this is boring. I'm not interested.

Yvonne: For myself, I'm like the exact opposite of that because I find the technical classes more interesting as opposed to the management classes. So I think I'm more with the [information] classes for a major. So, the classes I've taken so far are like the networking one, which I find more interesting. But on the other hand [the professional issues course] is more ... I've taken management and it's not all that exciting.

Mary: I don't really know yet. I guess I do like the technical side more but I couldn't be behind a desk all my life. I'm more of a people person. You can't just have management these days, you have to have something else, and a technology background looks really good on a resume.

Both Dara and Mary refer to "sitting behind a desk" as one of the characteristics of work that is more technologically intensive, and Mark referred to "sitting in a cubicle." You will find, however, that in the upcoming chapters, our working professionals put that myth to rest: Both technical and nontechnical jobs have a certain amount of desk work. The factors that determine how much desk work a person does have more to do with the organization's mission and each department's role than with the technical focus or nontechnical focus of the job.

However, the appearance of this myth in Dara's and Mary's comments does show that students have obtained a range of ideas about what information jobs are all about from various sources. Sometimes those ideas are accurate, and sometimes they are less so. In the same focus group as was excerpted above, we heard the following opinions:

Yvonne: I see [the information profession] as like, consulting, like integrating technology with different aspects of our daily lives, like businesses and that type of stuff. Consulting work, even creating programs, dealing with it in that sense.

Felicia: I agree with that. I want to be a librarian, and it's more of how people interact with information and getting them the information than necessarily the programming and the networking, but I think probably the interaction between people and the computers and getting information.

Dara: I would say IT basically is a tool for everyone to use to make [computers] user friendly, and I also think that it's mainly to help us. I carry my laptop around, like it's handy you know. And things we use in everyday life like the ATM. But actually when I leave here, I don't want to do anything technical, per se, but the [organizational behavior] class I'm in right now, it's helping me to realize all the managerial things that we're doing. The programming class [web development], I actually hated it the first time I was in there, but I actually like it now because we learn how people sit down and actually make a website, but that's not what I want to do when I leave. I don't want to do anything technical. I don't think technology is bad per se, but I don't see myself sitting in front of a computer all day long. I don't know exactly what IT professionals do—I don't know if they do code all day.

Mary: Basically what they're trying to say is you can, with the experience and background you're acquiring, you're going to be an IT professional, but an IT professional is not only that person that does programming, it could be any type of person that applies that knowledge to whatever function of a company or organization or whatever is their career … I always knew I wanted to be in the business world, definitely involving computers, not necessarily with the technical side, but with the management and the information and the computers. I took a certification class last year and that helped me decide that this was definitely something I wanted to do. I'm more into the hands-on aspect of this major as opposed to just sitting. Like [the networking class] last year was like textbook work and I can't get involved in the technical side unless I start doing things hands-on.

These students have focused on one part of the spectrum of information professions having to do with the mixture of "managerial" activities versus technology-related activities. The idea of "managerial versus technical" limits our thinking, however, in that it assumes that these two activities are opposed to each other and that the only reason for interacting with people is to "manage" them. Some jobs in the information professions trend heavily toward working directly with people in ways that have little or nothing to do with managing them. For instance, system analysts spend a substantial proportion of their time meeting with the end users who depend upon a particular IT tool. When accountants need their financial system to perform some new task, they describe their needs to a system analyst. Even IT project managers are not all about "managing" other people: Many project managers focus their efforts primarily on planning, tracking, and analyzing rather than on directing the work of other people. In the same vein, an information job involving a balance of regular contact with people and working with technology is the IT audit function. IT auditors collect and analyze information about how users actually work with information systems, in order to make sure that information is handled safely, securely, and efficiently. Finally, there is a whole group of jobs with the primary focus of helping other people to organize and locate information. These professionals create and provide information services, develop digital repositories of information, and invent structures to keep information organized. Their jobs typically have "librarian" in the title, but rather than working behind a desk in the local public library, many of them work with other information and technology professionals in corporations, governments, and schools. The important common feature across all of these jobs is that they may have little focus on technology per se and lots of involvement with people, but it's not necessarily in a "managerial" capacity.

On the technology side of the spectrum, there are other jobs in the information professions where working with software, devices, and systems on a daily basis forms the core of the job. For example, a database designer translates the design requirements provided by the system analyst into a working database system. This work involves configuring database software, writing queries (highly structured requests for information from a database system), designing reports, maintaining database security, as well as myriad hands-on tasks with computers. A substantial amount of interaction with other people is required to test and deploy the resulting database, but the frequent use of database tools is a dominant aspect of this job. However, jobs in the information field often fall in the middle by offering a mix of technical activities and people activities. For example, at the time Karen was interviewed as a senior, she had expertise in databases, information security, and web interfaces, but her skills went beyond these technical areas:

> So you could learn how to program a database in your database course, but learning how to apply all that in a business environment, answering the questions that the business needs answered, and drawing and manipulating data is a different story … I think the biggest thing in class was practicing management skills, how to work with people, and also how to find information because IT is changing so quickly, you have to learn how to learn, where to find information, where to go for it, for the latest technical reviews and management practices … The IT classes helped you learn how to learn.

We found these to be recurring themes in our interviews. Learning specific technical skills—for instance, how to write a database query—was an important kind of training, but the real educational value of a degree in the information field came from a much larger perspective than any particular set of technical skills. First, what Karen refers to as "learning how to learn" is a critical component of education in IT because the field changes very rapidly. IT consists of masses of machines designed by people, and there are so many people and companies and research labs at work that new technology is emerging all of the time. Having an aptitude for lifelong learning is important because innovations never stop in the information field. The second issue Karen described was "practicing management skills," and she elaborated on that a bit later:

> People are usually scared of IT people: They speak a foreign language, and they are not going to be able to help you, they are going to talk in techie terms. And I think that is the big thing, the biggest thing in overcoming when you are an IT person: You have to be personable obviously, but you have to learn how to translate technical terms, servers and networking and all those different terminologies to another employee that you are working with and trying to make the same ends on a project and trying to get them to give you the data that you need to translate it into SQL … I think that the biggest thing that I know I am going to have to encounter when I am in my next position is trying to be that translator.

This role of being a translator or serving as a bridge between individuals with a primary focus on business and those with a primary focus on technology is a largely overlooked, but it is a critically important position in organizations. The complexity of technology demands that some people master the intricacies of specific areas (such as the design of wireless networks). However, those specialists do not have the breadth of expertise to be able to solve business problems with technology. On the other hand, many businesspeople know what problems they need to solve, but they don't have the detailed understanding of the capabilities of the internet, databases, servers, networks, storage, and processing to be able to analyze the problem, establish the architecture of a solution, and communicate that architecture to technology specialists. Information professionals, like Karen, Grant, Anna, and Cayla, have all of those skills, *and* they have the ability to communicate clearly with people on both sides of the equation: the business leaders and the technology specialists. This role of translator or bridge between the domain of the problem (the business problem, or medical problem, or military problem, or government problem) and the domain of the solution (the necessary technology) is a key function of the information professional and the main focus of educational programs in the information field.

One additional idea that follows is that individuals who gain expertise in information management, information technology, information organization, or other areas *plus* some knowledge of another topic can provide irreplaceable value to the organizations in which they work. The authors of this book have worked with many students who study information *and* business, information *and* biology, information *and* journalism; these students are always more prepared and flexible than those who study just one topic. Combining information with another specialty topic gives them the opportunity to make career moves unavailable to other people. Senior student Germain shed light on the idea that education in IT can provide a gateway into other jobs:

> I think that you have to be able to mix a number of different backgrounds and education together for IT to be at the level where I want to be. I really see myself being deeply involved in different aspects of business, and I think that IT is probably one of the more important parts of that business because a lot of people can say they want to develop ... this interface for an idea that they have ... but

they have someone else do it for them, develop that portal. With my background I can actually develop prototypes in different programs myself. You don't have to go look for someone else to do that so one of the main advantages of having an IT background is that I've been immersed in that technology already. And I already have that training. A lot of people don't already have it, and I think that a lot of employers right now are looking for people that have technology background no matter what field you are going to … And, you know, it's very helpful for a lot of companies. But in terms of where I want to be, I think it does not stop here … But I think that IT is … I'm glad that IT [is] going to help me do a lot of different things that I want to do in the future.

Germain's response uncovers an interesting point of which many people are unaware: Immersive knowledge of technology is a new kind of literacy, nearly as fundamental as the ability to read and to use mathematics. Armed with that literacy—a clear and detailed understanding of how communication networks, databases, applications, and user interfaces work together—a person is prepared to perform a wide range of jobs at a level that surpasses those workers whose technology literacy is not so high. Germain notes that if he has a business idea that he wants to explore, he is capable of prototyping it himself. This highlights an important distinction between simply knowing how to use a technology and the ability to create innovative new products or services based on a rich understanding of how a technology works. This same point hit home for us in a recent conversation with a colleague who spoke with a student after an exam in an information technology class. The student could not understand why he had performed so poorly on the exam. He strongly felt that he had attained a strong mastery of IT, and he gave as an example the fact that he was highly familiar with all of the functions in his smartphone. Given the complexity of many of the gadgets we have adopted into our lives and the difficulty that some people have using them, it is perhaps not surprising to have a feeling of accomplishment from untangling the user interface of a poorly designed device. But it is important not to confuse mastery of gadgets with the knowledge, skills, and abilities needed to innovate and create a new product or service with technology. Research has shown that, in many areas of technology, students believe they are more competent than they actually are (Grant, Malloy, & Murphy, 2009). Germain's comments showed that he appreciated the importance of having the skills and knowledge to proceed smoothly from imagination to prototype.

Collectively, our student interviewees described a rich picture of their educational and preprofessional experiences. The fact that all of these students had participated in internships was no coincidence: Most jobs in the information professions are highly applied, and the education leading up to those jobs optimally has a strong hands-on component to it. Possibly the most exciting report from our student interviewees was the extent to which they saw the information field as a "people profession." Many of our respondents commented on how much they enjoyed the human interaction involved in working with information and technology. Students saw the business activities and processes involved in helping users solve their information challenges to be just as central to the success of an enterprise as finance or human resources. In the next chapter, we will compare and contrast the impressions of these students with those of working professionals to see how well the excitement and promise of a career in information persist into the working world.

Endnotes

1. Our research received Institutional Review Board approval for interviewing and video- or audio-taping research participants at Syracuse University. In this approval process, we agreed to seek explicit permission from each interviewee to use recordings and transcripts for research and educational purposes. Each individual whose words and description appear in this chapter gave this permission. We use pseudonyms to refer to each student.

References

Grant, D. M., Malloy, A. D., & Murphy, M. C. (2009). A comparison of student perceptions of their computer skills to their actual abilities. *Journal of Information Technology Education, 8,* 141–160.

CHAPTER 7

Barriers and Challenges: The Student Perspective

At this very moment, the fate of Iran is strangely entwined with the sleep schedules of the geeks who maintain the servers at Twitter and YouTube.

—Comedian John Hodgman, speaking at
the Radio and Television Correspondents
Association Dinner, June 19, 2009

Germain, one of the students we discussed in Chapter 6, had a summer internship in the information technology (IT) department of a large financial services company. We asked him whether he had encountered problems in "selling" the value of his educational background, and he told us the following:

> I think that having an information technology major has kind of been difficult because not a lot of places really understand what this major is, what it is you do. But you can prove yourself with your GPA and experiences that you've had on your own, that you are capable of even being considered for a position. Once you've been … well, at least, when I've got into an interview situation and you explain yourself, and you explain what the major has taught you, people love that. Employers love that … So I think the barrier is having people say "You're not a finance

major, you're not an accounting major, we can't even look
at your resume." And to me, I think that it's crazy.

Germain's experience suggests that other people's lack of understanding of the job roles in the field creates a barrier to professional
progress for those who major in IT or a related field. In Chapter 6, we
heard from students who had chosen the information field because
they wanted to work with technology itself and/or they wanted
involvement in the nontechnical, people-oriented aspects of the
field, such as project management, IT audit, systems analysis, or
librarianship. Earlier in the book, we explored the future demand for
jobs in the information fields, as well as the reasons some jobs could
be outsourced while others could not. Taken altogether, the picture
for information professionals seems quite good, with a diverse range
of students headed for interesting jobs that mix technology with
helping people. Rather than paint an unrealistic picture, however, it
is important to point out that students and workers in the information professions face a number of important challenges. In this chapter, we hear comments from students who can shed some light on
barriers they have faced or expect to face as they make the transition
to becoming information professionals.

Germain's comment earlier in this chapter concerns an important
point for students considering a career in the information field:
Public understanding of the profession has not caught up with the
reality of the wide range of roles in which information professionals
are involved. Many people understand to some degree what a programmer does or what a computer engineer does, but they may have
little understanding of how information professionals solve important and difficult problems by applying technology to them. Other
students had similar comments, as demonstrated in the following
quotes:

People can't figure out if it's business or computer science.
It's different. Most don't know what [the information field]

is. If it's computer related then that must mean programming. This scares people.

[In high school] we did not know there [was] something between computer science and management.

My mother doesn't have a clue what IT is. As people get older, they don't know what to "make" of this major. People don't think there are options.

Several students mentioned this difficulty of explaining the information field to family members. Parents and others who are unaware of the richness and variety of the field tended to have concerns about the employability of their children after they graduate with a major in IT or a related field, as expressed in the following comments:

People are scared of outsourcing, they hear it in the media. There are no jobs.

There isn't a need for entry-level people. There are established IT people in the company—many of us can't work our way in.

Because the IT field is constantly changing, people are afraid that they can't keep up with it and decide to go to more secure and stable jobs.

This field is constantly changing. Can't keep up. By the end of two years you will be out of a job. Have to keep updated.

The last two comments reflect an issue that we encountered earlier in the book: IT changes very quickly. Competitive pressures and constant innovation contrive to force technology companies into releasing the latest and greatest operating system, web technology, database, or security scanner at faster and faster rates. Some students see this pace of change as daunting, while others see it as a way to keep their jobs interesting. Those individuals willing to continually update knowledge and skills in their specialty may have a competitive advantage in the job marketplace, while those who prefer not to dig deeply into a dynamic technology area can move into roles that involve working with users, managing others, and organizing information resources with existing, stable technological tools.

So certain barriers to professional progress in the information field—lack of public awareness of the roles, resistance from family members who may misunderstand the field, and the high rate of technological change—are amenable to easy solutions. Greater awareness of the field is emerging over time, and the many career successes of recent graduates will reassure worried parents. Rapid technological change shows no sign of abating, but everyone in the field has to cope with the same problems of keeping up with changes, and the constant change creates new work opportunities for those who stay current.

Other challenges in the information field are not so easily rectified. Surveys we conducted in 2002 and 2003 on challenges to education in the IT sector indicated that students of color faced race-related barriers to their educational and professional progress in the information professions. Not all students experienced these barriers, as senior IT student Grant described:

> I haven't seen any barriers for someone like me, as of color. I mean my father is white and my mother is African American, so people ask me if I've ever had any issue with that. Have I ever experienced racism or anything like that, and I've never had anything like that at all, and coming to this school was so deep into diversity and to a school that's open to everyone. I've never seen any problems …

But Grant's positive experiences are not shared by everyone. Michelle, who was a junior when we interviewed her, was majoring in IT and minoring in finance. Before she started college, she had an internship at an insurance company. Michelle commented that on that internship, no one in her company really understood her cultural background:

> There [weren't] a lot of people of color in that environment. And this is where I was working, at headquarters, and there weren't a lot of black people at headquarters to begin with. So if someone happened to see me walking throughout the headquarters, and they weren't black, or Spanish, or Asian, I just felt like they were just gaping at you, or looking at you like, "What are you doing here?" It just felt really uncomfortable, and the environment was very … it was very serious, it wasn't too relaxed, they didn't warm up to you easily, which made it more difficult as a result.

Later in the interview, Michelle commented more specifically on her feelings of being a woman of color in the technology field:

> I would probably say that in addition to being a woman, being a woman of color is even harder because honestly we still have racism going on in today's society. Racism is prevalent in the corporate setting. It may not be as open, but it is still there, it still exists. I actually have seen it sometimes on the job in my internships … I might start my own business, trying to get students at a young age to be more interested in technology, not to be afraid of barriers that we may have to face. Because I look at it like this, that if you break this barrier now, you make it easier for a person that looks like you that's going to come up in that setting and I think that's the goal.

Being a woman of color in an IT job was a double concern for Michelle, in part because there were few other African Americans in her workplace, but also in part because some IT departments employ few or no women. Another of our interviewees, Lisha, originally from

Nigeria, reported that she and another female intern were the only women in her department during her internship. When we asked her how she felt about working in an environment that was predominantly male, she told us the following:

> It did not really faze me. I did not know if it is because I grew up with brothers, so I was not bothered, [or] because the other intern was female. I did not really look at it, but it did make me wonder if this is how it is going to be [for the rest of my career] … because if it is like that I would not feel comfortable … it makes me see that we are different, OK, I am the only female here, and so I have to make sure that, you know, I have to work twice as hard in a way, just because it is male dominated.

So Lisha seems to have adapted to the situation at her internship, although she questioned whether on an ongoing basis she would have to work harder in order to get respect in an IT department, simply because she was the only woman. She reported a similar situation with an engineering class she took:

> First of all, I was the only female in the class, I was the only African-American female in the class, and I did not want to give up, you know, I didn't want to say OK, I am going to drop this class because you know, [the professor] was not going to help me. So I really was just working extra hard, many nights I spent [studying], I had to take more time to learn it. What was good for me was there were students in the class who wanted to help … I did find students to help me, that was really a good thing for me …

Lisha's experience both in the classroom and on her internship confirms an aspect of technology-intensive workplaces that is, unfortunately, not unusual. These environments commonly have a greater number of men than women and a greater number of whites (in U.S.

organizations). Although Lisha reported that co-workers and students were supportive of her success, dealing with the unbalanced gender mix required some adaptation.

The importance of having a supportive work environment was also critical in the internship of Anna, a senior IT major:

> The internship that I had was in New York, a place I want to work in the near future [and it was at] one of world's leading consulting companies. It has different services for its clients, like investigations, business intelligence investigation; they do forensic accounting ... I interned under the IT department. Basically, when I interned there, it was like a reality hitting on my face just because I know from my [educational] background, the number of females in the classroom is very, very low. But I guess I am already accustomed to it. And now I am trying my way to stand out. So, going to the working environment and actually experiencing that in the corporate world, OK, it's really real. So, once I entered the office, I was introduced to the whole department. The department was pretty small. It's only six of them including the director ... all of them were males. And, they were all older than me, like twenty, ten years older than me, wow, so it was a big age gap. And, just being the only female, I first felt it was kind of rough, just because they still tried to get to know me and I tried to get to know them. All the conversation was based on like, I guess, man stuff, sports, and all that stuff. I was like, that I have nothing to say about that, however, I never found it uncomfortable there. They welcomed me and slowly I became an extra member of the little family there. And later on, I realized I loved to work at that company, or to be part of a company that has that culture, that working environment. I fell in love with them. I still stay in contact with them; I miss them; they said they will be missing me too.

The female students we interviewed had all faced and overcome some of the challenges related to women being underrepresented, particularly in the more technical areas of the information world. So while the bad news is that there is still more progress needed in achieving gender equity, the good news is that the educational and work environments encountered by these students often proved warm and supportive to the inclusion of women. The picture was much more mixed with respect to the experiences of underrepresented minorities. Although these students generally had positive experiences on campus, U.S. workplaces still suffer from overt and covert racism. Researcher Eileen Trauth (Trauth, Huang, Quesenberry, & Morgan, 2007) and her colleagues (Tapia, Kvasny, & Trauth, 2004) have clearly documented the relative dearth of women and underrepresented minorities in both educational and professional settings in the information systems and information technology fields. Trauth documented statistics showing that the percentage of African Americans in the IT workforce fell from 9.1 percent to 8.1 percent in the seven-year period ending in 2002. As long as these shortages of women and minorities persist in the information fields, we will continue to have uncomfortable work settings where anyone who is not a white male might feel somewhat out of place.

Part of the reason that some areas of the information professions have historically been unappealing to women and minorities may lie in the stereotypes that are applied to those who are interested in technology. Very few people live their school experiences without being labeled in some way, but young people with an inclination to excel at science, technology, engineering, or math have been particularly vulnerable, as the slings and arrows of high school misfortune sometimes affect those who work hard and achieve academically. While the most common names are nerd and geek, a variety of other choice slurs, such as dweeb, dork, weenie, grind, gearhead, and brainiac, are sometimes thrown in for good measure. The battered copy of the 1991 *Random House Webster's College Dictionary* in our research lab defines *geek* as any strange or eccentric person and *nerd* as a person dedicated to a nonsocial pursuit. Wikipedia updates the definition of a *nerd* with a somewhat more positive spin: A "person who passionately pursues intellectual activities, esoteric knowledge, or other obscure interests rather than engaging in more social or popular activities."[1]

To some, these labels may seem harmless enough—as a way for adolescents to sort out their social order on the way to adulthood. Despite this possibility, we wondered whether the application of these labels and the stereotypes that went with them might have an influence on what activities students chose to pursue in high school. If so, that might also influence what majors they might be prepared to undertake in college. In short, we wondered if the use of geek and nerd as epithets might not serve as a barrier for those who might have intrinsic interest in pursuing math and science.

To answer this question, we surveyed 53 undergraduates, asking them about a profile of a hypothetical student who was a high achiever in a technical discipline. The profile described the high-achieving student and related a scenario in which the student was labeled by an acquaintance. In about half of the cases, the high-achieving student was a male, given the name Paul, and in the other half a female, Mary. Each of these halves was further subdivided into a group in which the acquaintance called the student a geek or nerd and another group in which the student was not labeled by the acquaintance. We then posed two questions to the students who participated in the study: 1) If you were at a party, would you talk with Paul/Mary, and 2) could you see yourself being friends with Paul/Mary? In keeping with typical survey practice, we averaged the responses to the two questions to get a more reliable score indicating the likability of the high-achieving student, Paul or Mary, who was described in the scenario.[2]

Our analysis showed a distinctive pattern that depended upon whether the high-achieving student depicted in the scenario was female or male. Overall, if you were a high-achieving student such as the ones depicted in our study, it would be better to be male than female. Ignoring whether or not he was called a geek or a nerd, Paul was always seen as somewhat more likable than Mary. Interestingly, however, this relatively small difference hid a more important complexity. When the depicted student was Paul, the survey respondents described his likability as roughly the same whether or not he had been labeled as a geek or nerd. In contrast, when the high achiever was Mary, the survey respondents rated her as *more* likable when the stereotypic label was applied. In short, being a high-achieving female student was disadvantageous overall in terms of likability, but if you were a high-achieving female, it might actually be better if your friends labeled you as a geek.

We noticed among the male students we interviewed a general lack of concern about having the geek or nerd label applied to them. A bit later in our interview with student Grant, we asked him if he'd ever been called a geek or a nerd and if that label bothered him at all, to which he told us the following:

> Yes I have, but you know I have no issue with that because when their computers need to be fixed, I'm the first one to call. So you've got to take it with a shrug. So it really doesn't bother me. If I'm going to be called a geek or a nerd then I guess that's what I am, but as long as I am able and happy with what I'm doing, it doesn't make a difference. A label doesn't bother me. I see no negative connotation in it. There could be negative connotations in the term geek or nerd, but it just means someone who is focused in what they're doing and knows a lot about a general subject.

In contrast, when we asked female students about the label, they described a more involved process of realizing how they might involve themselves in the information professions without having the geek or nerd stereotype apply to them. We asked the question about geeks and nerds to Fiona, a senior student who as a freshman was waitlisted for a major in broadcast journalism and ended up in an IT major as her backup. In the following comments, Fiona describes her initial conception of the information professions after she failed to get into her preferred major, journalism, and instead had to start her college career in an alternative major, information technology:

> I love dealing with people, and that's why I figured broadcast journalism would be a great way to interact. And when I first came here, I was miserable ... My parents actually told me to put a smile back on my face, or they'd turn the car around and head back home. I thought it was a geek's major; I thought that everybody wound up working overseas; you'd never have a job market here in the United States—very stereotypical things that I had heard. And when I took [the introductory course], it was more about how the use of information builds successful businesses and helps them acquire clients. And it's not sitting behind a computer, and that it's not just geeks or coding ... all the stereotypes just kind of flew away. But it was also ... it was such a futuristic tone of opportunity, there was just so much left open for study ... And what I've learned [will] catapult me into a career with pretty much endless opportunity. So it finally just started to make sense when I saw that IT was everywhere ... and it just kind of made sense as a viable career choice.

The women who were comfortable with being labeled as a geek or nerd had sometimes arrived at that position not because of their involvement in technology, but rather, because they were high achievers. When we asked another senior information technology student about whether her friends ever called her a geek in high school, she confirmed that fact in the following comments:

> Not because I liked computers. It was because I was intelligent and got good grades. That was why I was called a geek or a nerd. I don't ever think it was applied to my technical knowledge.

This quote was from Karen, a young woman who subsequently graduated with highest honors from her college. Karen suggested that being labeled as a geek or a nerd had more to do with simply being a high academic achiever and not particularly because of her association with technology. This is a bit dispiriting because it suggests an anti-achievement aspect of high school student culture that situates intelligent girls at a disadvantage. In the focus groups we ran with first- and second-year college students, we heard the following range of similarly depressing stereotypes about females and the information professions:

> Girls aren't into math and science. Girls aren't into computers.

> Girls aren't into fixing things—like cars and computers. They just enjoy using them.

> Women look at social sciences, not the pure sciences.

> Most people think females can't relate to math.

> Girls aren't interested in how computers work.

These comments, all from female students, were stereotypes that these students had heard other people express about girls' interest and ability in technical and scientific topics. We did not hear any similar sentiments about minority students, perhaps because the overt expression of such stereotypes would be seen as racist, but there is ample evidence in the research literature documenting the presence and impact of such stereotypes (Tapia & Kvasny, 2004). Researchers Donald Chinn and Tammy VanDeGrift conducted an experiment on student beliefs about what made a software engineer hirable and found evidence that women and Hispanic job candidates were seen as having less desirable characteristics for software work (Chinn & VanDeGrift, 2008). These kinds of stereotypes, though seemingly harmless in an experiment on hiring in a fictional company, may have a profound influence on what careers schoolchildren believe are suitable for them.

In one study, conducted among 1,482 Maryland families with students in high school (Zarrett & Malanchuk, 2005), researchers found that students "who believed they were good at computers, had taken IT courses, and were encouraged by influential others were likely to be pursuing an IT career, whereas those with negative schemas about people who use computers were not" (p. 71). In this context, a schema is a set of related beliefs: for example, that people who use computers are antisocial. In the case of minority students, these adverse stereotypes combine with a very tangible lack of resources to make a career in the information professions much more challenging to achieve. In a national study a few years ago, Karen Mossberger and her colleagues (2006) found that although young African Americans had just as positive an attitude toward IT as whites, those who grew up in poorer communities had considerably less access to IT all the way through high school. The problem is not always a lack of equipment but often the unavailability of trained teachers who can lead students through the most sophisticated uses of the technology (Wenglinsky, 1998).

Combine these resource deficiencies with the stereotypes that portray IT and related areas as the sole domain of geeky white males and the result is a sure formula for discouraging girls and minority students from participation in the information professions. The following excerpt from a 2003 report from the Information Technology Association of America sums up the situation quite powerfully:

> Information technology is often portrayed in movies and books as a solitary and anti-social profession, dominated primarily by young, white males. The phrases "computer geek" or "computer nerd" are well entrenched in the popular culture. These images certainly ignore the fact that software is often developed in teams, in highly collaborative settings, where intellect and motivation are most likely to determine one's standing with both peers and managers.

Still, these negative images of the inept technophile may be another barrier that may be deterring females and minorities from the high tech industry. Females and minorities may feel isolated or unaccepted in the IT profession and, therefore, may choose other career fields that are less technical or sectors where there are greater numbers of minorities. (Report of the ITAA blue ribbon panel on IT diversity, 2003, p. 6)

Take heart, however, for all is not lost. One side effect of the explosion of the use of IT in business, government, and education is that new job roles have sprung up faster than can ever possibly be filled by geeky white males. In the next two chapters, we explore the professional world of information from the perspective of men and women who work there. These perspectives will show that such a huge range of knowledge, skills, and outlooks is required across the many job roles in the information field that the old stereotypes about the boys' club in the computer room no longer apply in the emerging marketplace of information jobs.

Endnotes

1. Accessed from Wikipedia (en.wikipedia.org/wiki/Nerd).
2. Detailed statistical procedures and results are available on request from the authors.

References

Chinn, D., & VanDeGrift, T. (2008). Uncovering student values for hiring in the software industry. *Journal on Educational Resources in Computing (JERIC)*, *7*(4).

Information Technology Association of America. (2003). *Report of the ITAA blue ribbon panel on IT diversity*. Presented at the national IT workforce convocation, Arlington, VA.

Mossberger, K., Tolbert, C. J., & Gilbert, M. (2006). Race, place, and information technology. *Urban Affairs Review, 41*(5), 583.

Tapia, A. H., & Kvasny, L. (2004). Recruitment is never enough: Retention of women and minorities in the IT workplace. *Proceedings of the SIGMIS Conference on Computer Personnel Research: Careers, Culture, and Ethics in a Networked Environment*, 84–91.

Tapia, A. H., Kvasny, L., & Trauth, E. M. (2004). Is there a retention gap for women and minorities? The case for moving in versus moving up. *Strategies for managing IS/IT personnel*, 153–164.

Trauth, E. M., Huang, H., Quesenberry, J. L., & Morgan, A. J. (2007). Leveraging diversity in information systems and technology education in the global workplace. *Information Systems and Technology Education: From the University to the Workplace*, 27.

Wenglinsky, H. (1998). *Does it compute? The relationship between educational technology and student achievement in mathematics*. Princeton, NJ: Educational Testing Service.

Zarrett, N. R., & Malanchuk, O. (2005). Who's computing? Gender and race differences in young adults' decisions to pursue an information technology career. *New Directions for Child and Adolescent Development* (110).

CHAPTER 8

The Workplace Perspective on the Information Field

A man who works with his hands is a laborer; a man who works with his hands and his brain is a craftsman; but a man who works with his hands and his brain and his heart is an artist.
—Louis Nizer, English lawyer

So let's say the time has come to look for a new job. Here are some required qualifications from a high-paying job recently advertised in the Bethesda, Maryland, area. The job offers health insurance, four weeks of vacation, transportation benefits, and a retirement plan. The following skills and experience are required:

- Web and database management skills and experience
- Ability to communicate via listserv, blog, wiki, and other internet tools
- Ability to create and edit materials such as project reports, budgets, and proposals
- Professional or volunteer experience in emergency preparedness and response
- Knowledge or experience working with first responders and health professionals
- Experience as an informationist

The last item in the list might raise the question of what an informationist is. Frank Davidoff, former editor of *Annals of Internal Medicine*, and his colleague appear to have coined the term as it is commonly used today in an editorial published in 2000. Davidoff claimed the term for the area of medicine and healthcare and described it as an information specialist who "play[s] a crucial role in improving existing information retrieval systems and creating new ones by finding out more about when and how clinicians, patients, and families need information, what information they need most, and in what forms it is most useful to them" (p. 998). Perhaps the most interesting aspect of this job description, however, is the three-way combination of information skills (e.g., the web, databases, wikis, and others), people skills (communication, working with first responders), and experience with emergency preparedness and response. This combination evokes a sense of excitement in bringing together the latest internet-based information tools with the mission critical area of emergency response.

By the way, it may be surprising to learn that this combination of skills and experience was advertised with the job title of Medical Librarian, and the preferred educational background was either in library science or information science. (Note that these two areas are frequently combined in a single degree program titled Library and Information Science.)

The combination of skills, the surprising title, and the excellent pay and benefits are three characteristics that highlight the unusual and diverse possibilities for jobs in the information professions. The common element that binds together the range of jobs in the information professions is the central concern for provision of organized and meaningful information to the end users. Under this umbrella, experts distinguish between those whose work focuses more on infrastructure and those whose work focuses more on services. Infrastructure in this context refers to basic hardware for information communication, storage, processing, and presentation, plus the essential software that binds that equipment together. Running on top of that infrastructure, applications and services provide the end users with the information and tools they need to perform their jobs. A veteran information system professional, Richard,[1] who worked in a healthcare context, described this division in the following way:

> I started part-time while I was in college in the [medical] records department, and then I stayed full-time after that. A few years later they implemented the medical records system in the department, so I stayed on and become the department systems coordinator in medical records. Then I attained my current position here in information services, which is manager of information services. We have our two distinct sections: One is the IT side ... information technology, they handle all the networking, the infrastructure, and the data center, most of the security, especially the network security: Then there's the IS [information systems] side of things, which I manage; they're mostly [the] application side project management, integration of our applications, some security—application-side security issues.

Richard's quote highlights a continuing terminology problem in the information professions where one term can mean more than one thing in different contexts. In particular, *information systems*, or IS, can refer to individual computers, groups of computers connected by networks, computers and software working together, or the name of a college major generally located within business schools. Likewise, *information technology*, or IT, can also refer to one or more computers, a smaller device such as a cell phone, infrastructure such as networks, or a college major often located in a school of engineering or technology.

Many of the job characteristics of information professionals are common across different organizations, but the specific role of each information professional is highly variable, similar to other professions. For example, all doctors study medicine, but after they complete a specialty, they perform their jobs within pediatrics, oncology, etc. In addition to their specialty area, doctors are also employed in a wide variety of organizational types: traditional medical practices, forensics departments, insurance companies, state and federal government, the military, or in an educational environment. The same diversity holds within the information professions. Not only are there dozens of different specialty roles, but a person who has specialized in any given area, such as telecommunications or digital libraries, would have opportunities in a wide range of different organizational settings (i.e., not just high-tech companies or public libraries).

When we asked experienced information professionals what to say to young people about their jobs, our interviewee Anne offered the following, which we found quite important:

> Knowing *how* to use technology is important, but the real skill is to use technology to identify information needs, research, organize, communicate, and solve problems. Creating lists of specific tasks utilizing technology, by itself, will not move us toward meaningful information and technology literacy. Applying a set of technology skills in different contexts, situations, and actually solve problems represents authentic life skills. Most of us that have been in the workforce for more than 10 years have seen that the skills we need to survive constantly change—the pace of this change is accelerating. Web-based technology not only allows us more direct access to sources of information that are continually changing, they expand the walls of our schools, libraries, and even home offices and play spaces. Information technology has become a necessary department in most businesses today due to the prevalence of the internet and computer-based networks providing the basis of all database storage and communications in organizations. Information technology is a highly competitive field, and the best way to be competitive and realize your career potential is to study for an information technology major.

Certainly, the information professions are directly impacted by rapid changes in information technologies, so the job of information professional requires constant adaptation to new hardware and software that affects the jobs and organizations. As stated by Sandra, one of the professionals we interviewed, it is part of her job to enjoy change:

> The one thing being in IT is [that] it's forever changing, forever changing. If you think you've learned something, forget it because they've changed it the next month and you're going to learn it all over again. So if you don't like learning new things and you don't like change, this isn't the job for you. That's guaranteed.

Information professionals tend to be self-motivated and are conscious of the importance of the knowledge that they constantly need to acquire. Many respondents reported feeling enthusiastic or even joyful at the prospect of learning a new system or procedure and confident in their skill at obtaining the new knowledge:

> I am learning as I go with all of this. I love to learn. That's the most important part I think.

> I just read books and figured it out.

This need to constantly update may also explain why some people avoid pursing these degrees. Sandra, who was previously quoted, said:

> I believe that most are afraid of the technology changes in the IT field. They believe that only the geeks get into the IT field and that is why some do not apply. I can say that I am not a math guru but I entered the IT field some 20 years ago and I have done an excellent job at it. However, having said that, the IT field is so broad, and it is forever changing. Once I learn a certain system, I have to continue to train,

study, and keep up with changing technology. I believe
that fear keeps most from entering the field.

Many information professionals work directly with end users to
help them solve their information problems. Depending upon the
nature of the task, relationships between information professionals
and end users can, in some cases, be highly collaborative. Our interviews captured several examples of satisfaction when information
professionals help users. As stated in the following quotes from an
academic setting, information professionals are aware of and enjoy
their helping role:

> I like the fact that a lot of people depend on us, all the
> departments. We contribute to what they do, and without
> us they would have more trouble in their jobs. I like that
> dependency.

> I feel needed. When I was first living in the dorms, I helped
> people with computers there all the time. I was known as
> the kid who could help you with your computer if you had
> problems with it. It was a great way to meet people. I
> would go in and fix their computer and get to know them
> while I was doing it.

Likewise, users usually appreciate the help they receive, the
patience with which it is delivered, and the sensitivity of IT staff to the
difficulty of learning new technical skills. The following quotes from
technology users at a large hospital indicate appreciation for the
assistance of the hospital's IT staff:

> She gets right to it and explains it to me.

> She writes everything down. I really need that.

> He's great. He doesn't talk over everyone's head, you know?

> I count on her (an IT staff member) in a lot of ways, not just the computer. It's almost all on her shoulders, so to speak … It must be difficult for her, having us on her case all the time.

This last quote recognizes the challenge of all helping professions: the fact that many people depend heavily upon the professionals who serve them. As a result, the responsibilities for a wide range of problems tend to fall on the shoulders of an information professional, particularly when they work in so-called front facing positions. A commonly held misconception about the information field lies in the lack of recognition and appreciation of this front facing position. From the perspective of someone who has only interacted with sales associates at computer stores or who has only seen the television caricature of the IT help desk geek, these front facing positions may seem like a joke. Without picking on a particular computer chain store, it seems that all too often, the (male) salespeople in these stores were hired primarily on their ability to throw around technology jargon rather than actually help people make a sensible choice about a computer purchase. And the help desk personnel depicted on shows such as *The Office* and in comic strips seem to get a perverse enjoyment out of confusing computer users and preventing them from doing their jobs. As our quotes have shown, real-life information professionals are rarely anything like these cartoonish misrepresentations. If they were, they would soon lose their jobs because businesses, hospitals, universities, and other organizations depend heavily on professionalism and their willingness to provide help and support to a range of users with a wide range of needs.

What these stereotypical representations of technology people also hide is that the information professions include a variety of roles and functions. Those individuals who have spent several years in the workplace have often become familiar with these varying roles, but those outside the information professions, particularly members of the general public, are often less well informed about the field. This lack of realistic, accurate information may be one of the factors leading to the stereotyping of information professionals into categories such as geek and nerd. One of our interviewees, Richard, indicated that he believed the reason there were relatively few women in the IT field is because they do not have good information about the available jobs, resulting in the impression that the technology aspects of the work are the most important parts of these jobs:

> I think that the perception of IT is all about machinery, and technology, and algorithms—very impersonal work. I think that the perception is that you will always be down on the floor under a lab table or under a desk connecting wires and fixing hardware. I don't want to speak in generalizations, but I think those type of fields are not very attractive to many females ... but I also want to say that it is not very attractive to me and I don't see the IT field like that. I see the IT field as something that you are working with people not computers and you are helping people use computers. And I think that is why we are seeing in our master's programs here [an information school] that MLIS, the library science program, tends to be predominately females, but that is the program that focuses more on the user side of things and the access of information and working with others. Our telecommunication program tends to be predominately male and that is because it tends to be perceived as [a] more network engineering sort of thing. However, I have seen some female students who have been absolutely brilliant in telecommunications and have seen some male students who are wonderful in library science. I cannot answer for you as to why one type of job is seen as for females and one type of job is for males. If I could answer that question, I think that I would be much better off. I would be a richer person too.

These stereotypes also figure into a widespread myth that was often emphasized during the so-called dot-com boom (1996–2001) and then punctured shortly thereafter. Specifically, some students in the late 1990s became interested in the information professions in part because of reports about very high salaries. Later, after the dot-com boom went bust, the opposite myth was publicized: An over-supply of information professionals had driven salaries down. We also talked with our interviewees about salary issues. Timothy, a new professional in the field, mentions that he entered the field because he was told that people in these jobs were well-paid. His actual experience, as explained in the following comment, shows that the pay was not as high as he expected but also that the demand for information professionals has been stable and only certain job types have been outsourced:

> I was told that the pay scale for IT would be much larger than that of an educator, which was my original intention … It is not that you can't make money in IT, but it is not a magic realm of high paying jobs, by any means … And I think that IT has become a commodity now. It is … a field that tends to be more contracted out, tends to be out-sourced. I think that where the opportunity in IT now is no longer the understanding of networking and fixing some-one's computer problem, that can be contracted out. Where the opportunity is? Making IT decisions for an organization and managing those projects on behalf of the organization you work for. Even if your project team [members] are all consultants, most organizations want somebody internally making those strategic decisions.

Indeed, salary statistics from the U.S. government confirm that salaries in the information professions have risen gradually over time, similar or sometimes slightly more than those in other professions such as finance, education, and healthcare. Any differences in salary growth between the information professions and other professions seem to have more to do with the location of the job and the industry the job is in. Career development researcher Sumati Srinivas (2009) studied the employment patterns of young workers and found that workers who move into high-tech industries from other industries are likely to obtain higher wages, even when taking into account differences in education levels and other related factors. Economic researcher Madeline Zavodny (2003) found that the only substantial difference between technology-intensive professions and other professions was that the jobs of college educated people in technology-intensive positions were more stable than the non-technology-intensive jobs. Zavodny concluded her article by suggesting that "skilled workers in technology-intensive industries may have more general skills that enable them to switch employers more easily than other workers" (Zavodny, 2003, p. 276).

This economic and career research, together with information we obtained from our interviewees, suggested that getting a job in the information field is not a get-rich-quick recipe. Those individuals who are primarily interested in making a lot of money quickly should probably look to Wall Street rather than the library or software company on Main Street. Instead, a person can think of the information professions as technology-rich places where there are many opportunities to help people solve their information problems in industry, education, healthcare, and other sectors. Collectively, our information professionals described a number of the reasons their jobs were interesting and challenging. Many college educated people believe that interest and challenge are key ingredients in a job that is enjoyable.

Our interviewees also mentioned how much they appreciate the degree to which others within their organizations value their roles. Because information professionals tend to have the deepest understanding of the workings of information and information technology within organizations, they influence a range of functions within the organization, including finances, human resources, security, logistics, employee training, and managerial decision making. The information professional is not necessarily an expert in any of these areas, but his or her expertise in providing the right information resources at the right time ensures that the value and importance of his or her role is well known in the organization. This factor—being appreciated and valued—is certainly another ingredient in a job that is satisfying and fulfilling.

On a related note, the information professionals we interviewed showed a detailed understanding of the human side of the information professions and were well aware that technology was just one aspect of their work. That many of the roles in the information professions are essentially helping roles is one of the key areas in which many members of the general public have a poor understanding of the field. Although there are certainly a variety of jobs that are highly technology-intensive and a number of others that are primarily concerned with ideas or data rather than with people, the vast majority of jobs in the information professions involve daily contact with end users. Much of this daily contact involves understanding the needs of these users and then helping to choose, configure, organize, and deploy the right combination of technologies to fulfill those needs. In this sense, some information professionals are much the same as architects and builders. Architects and builders find out the needs of users for the physical space in which they live and work. They then deploy a variety of technologies to create that space and make it work for the users. Likewise, many information professionals find out the needs of users of information. They then use information technologies and services to fulfill those needs. Just as physical spaces range from garden sheds to skyscrapers, information systems range from smartphones all the way to huge, interconnected systems that predict the weather or run the stock market. Along this spectrum, there are opportunities for people with a variety of interests, and in particular, some who have a strong affinity for technology and others who do not. Regardless of how much a person enjoys working hands-on with gadgets and devices, there is a challenging, interesting, valued, and "people-centric" position available somewhere in the information field.

With this optimistic perspective, it is easy to overlook the fact that working in an information profession can present a few pitfalls and a few hardships, particularly for women and members of underrepresented minorities who work in the more technology-intensive areas of the field. In the next chapter, we balance our optimistic overview here with a realistic preview of important challenges that some will face as they enter the information professions. We believe that students will benefit from this realistic perspective because, armed with accurate information in advance, they can prepare themselves mentally for the challenges they may encounter when they enter the workforce during an internship or their first position.

Endnotes

1. Our research received Institutional Review Board approval for interviewing research participants from organizations undergoing technology changes in 2001. Initial results of this study were reported in Guzman, Stam, and Stanton (2008). We have substituted pseudonyms in place of our interviewees' first names.

References

Davidoff, F., & Florance, V. (2000). The informationist: A new health profession? *American College* of Physicians, *132*, 996–998.

Guzman, I. R., Stam, K. R., & Stanton, J. M. (2008). The occupational culture of IS/IT personnel within organizations. *Data Base for Advances in Information Systems, 39*(1), 33–50.

Srinivas, S. (2009). The impact of technological mobility on workers' careers. *Career Development International, 14*(2), 133–147.

Zavodny, M. (2003). Technology and job separation among young adults, 1980–98. *Economic Inquiry, 41*(2), 264–278.

CHAPTER 9

Barriers and Challenges: The Workplace Perspective

Making ... an art out of your technological life is the
way to solve the problem of technology.
　　　　　—Robert M. Pirsig, author, *Zen and the Art of*
　　　　　Motorcycle Maintenance, NPR interview, 1974

Given the importance of effective use and manipulation of information in organizations today, the role played by those who are in charge of developing, implementing, maintaining, and supporting technology tools that can use this information to competitive advantage is crucial. Organizations constantly face the problem of hiring and retaining qualified information professionals who clearly understand the strategic role of information within the organization. Experts have identified several challenges when managing information professionals within organizations. Managing human resources in information technology (IT) differs in important ways from managing human resources in general because of the unique characteristics of the field, including rapid and continuous change and the newness of the profession. The information professions are not as well-established as other disciplines such as manufacturing or finance. Uncertainty about the expectations for information workers combines with ambiguity about the strategies for the use of information systems within organizations. Information professionals are still perceived by many managers as either techies or librarians who are in either case too far removed from the critical realities of the organization (Sadler, 1994). In the following quote, our interviewee Daniel talks about the variety of tasks that are understood to be part of this function:

> I am the Director of Information Systems, which is fondly known as "anything having to do with a plug" is my responsibility. So, it ranges from the network operations to setting up applications, setting up PCs, setting up an internal network, setting up the wide area network with [name of city], allowing dial-ins, assisting home users with dial-in, as well as all the telecommunications, the voicemail systems, the PBXs, the photocopiers—anything that's network dependent is my responsibility.

Among researchers, this situation is known as *role overload* because managers have placed upon Daniel's shoulders the responsibilities for a set of organizational activities that both vary widely and overlap only somewhat with each other. Although some people enjoy the challenge of such a diverse range of tasks, role overload can also lead to stress and burnout. Moore (2000) found that overload was the strongest contributor to exhaustion among technology workers. Our interviewee Mark talked about the level of demand in his job:

> [laughs aloud] It's very interesting. It's very demanding. My day, every day is different. There is always so much work to be done so if I wanted to spend 24 hours a day here, I could. It's a matter of saying enough is enough and going home.

In situations of role overload, it is also common to have more tasks to accomplish than one person (or one department) can possibly do along with minimal agreement among higher-level managers on the priorities among tasks. Researchers refer to this situation as role ambiguity. In situations of role ambiguity, a person can choose among many different possible tasks and has to set up daily goals for himself or herself. Another IT professional, Barbara, put it this way:

> You get up and start the day and say you are going to accomplish these five things, and it doesn't happen. And it might not happen the next day either, or the next, and that's where the conflict is. You try to set goals and think you are trying to meet them, but it's very difficult.

As is the case in other professions, research has shown that information professionals who experience high levels of work exhaustion also report greater intentions to leave their jobs (Moore, 2000). The constant flux of the technology creates some of the challenges that information professionals experience. In the following quote, our interviewee Clint indicated the technical issues that he felt were frustrating in his job:

> Yeah, there's a lot of frustrating things. Where do I start? I think the unreliable technology is very frustrating. You know with anything that someone is trying to sell you, everything that you read from the vendor and everything they tell you are the good stuff. The implementation is not as smooth as you would like to believe. But reliability of software is getting better. It's not so much of an issue today as it was two years ago.

Other interviews we conducted indicated that leading causes of stress, overload, and burnout were insufficient staff and resources, changes in technology and/or business environment, unrealistic deadlines and target dates, and organizational restructuring. One study of job satisfaction among IT workers, conducted by Mark McMurtrey and colleagues (2002) found that job stress often led to burnout and higher intentions among IT personnel to jump ship to another organization. Note that the best organizations—such as consulting firm Ernst & Young, technology company IBM, and financial services firm JPMorgan Chase—are highly aware of these research results, and they build human resource policies that help information workers (and people in other professions) try to avoid stress and burnout. Well-informed information professionals know that policies such as flextime, telecommuting, child care resources, stress reduction programs, and parental leave help make an employer more attractive.

Assuming a person can learn to thrive in situations that have some role overload and/or some role ambiguity and that one can avoid the twin pitfalls of stress and burnout, it is possible for an information professional to have a highly satisfying, flexible, and well-paying job. Many of the experienced professionals we interviewed show a great satisfaction about having a job in which they could continue their learning on a daily basis. In the previous chapter, we quoted Richard, who was an information systems manager overseeing two employees when he was asked about his position. On this topic, Richard said the following:

> I have a great position. I have learned so much, it's incredible. I get to do purchasing, database creation, support, [and] training is wonderful. What I am finding is that I like to do everything but I don't have time. So I really like my job, but I would like to be able to concentrate on some other things. That is why I try to delegate the support requests that come in.

Information professionals also face challenges at the workplace related to the technology itself, the work environment, and the professional context. We have mentioned in previous chapters how technology changes very rapidly over time; this creates a situation in which some information professionals must constantly update their technical knowledge about the devices, products, and services with which they work. What is less obvious, however, is that these technology changes modify the basic nature of information work by creating new work tasks, new job roles, and completely new career paths. For example, information security was a relatively minor concern in most industries until the internet began to extend the reach of viruses and other malicious software in the late 1980s and early 1990s. Due to recent extreme employment growth in the information security area, completely new job functions have been created, such as network security specialist, security administrator, and information systems auditor.

Changes in technology have even led to modification of the laws and regulations that govern how companies do business; this too has caused evolution of job roles. The U.S. legislation called the Sarbanes-Oxley Act of 2002 placed responsibility for reporting accurate accounting data on the managers and information professionals who work on the financial aspects of their companies. Implementation of this law caused scrutiny of IT practices involved in the accumulation, recording, and reporting of financial information. As a result, information professionals and their managers have had to increase the emphasis on the importance of developing communication skills and focusing on strategic business goals rather than purely on the technology itself. To be highly effective in their jobs, information professionals need to understand the strategic goals of the organization and how the management of information serves those goals. Information professionals whose skills are up to this task can also communicate the opportunities that effective information management can provide to their organizations. For example, Joseph explains in the following quote the importance of his role as information assurance administrator in the continuous operation of the business:

> My experience is that information assurance and network security are the growing areas of IT. Network planning is still a prerequisite, and the skills must continually evolve as the technology does; however, now more than ever [information assurance] is the critical piece to assuring [that] networks continue to operate efficiently and safely.

Note that information assurance is a broad term that encompasses information security but that also includes related areas such as business continuity planning, regulatory compliance, disaster recovery, certification, and accreditation. All of these are areas in which information professionals can play a very active role, and each of the areas also represents a bridge between management and the information professions. Because areas such as disaster recovery do cross over between very different job specialties (for example, business management and information technology), it is important to think about how information professionals obtain the interdisciplinary cross-training they need to be able to bridge these areas effectively. According to computer personnel researchers Fred Niederman and Jo Ellen Moore (2000), professional training, including specialization, continuing education, and retraining (that is, changing from one specialty area to another), is one of the most challenging activities that information professionals must wrestle with during their careers. At each point during their careers, information professionals must decide on what new skills to train, how to integrate the new learning on the job, and how to practice and reinforce what is learned. Particularly in smaller organizations, information professionals often need to learn much of the new technology they encounter on their own. IT department manager Steve reported that:

> For example, we are rolling out [a new version of] Windows
> [on our] workstations. We have not received training in
> that, so it's really what we have learned on our own.

In smaller organizations, there is often no special budget set aside for professional development or on-the-job training, so it is incumbent upon information professionals to be able to make their own time—sometimes at work, sometimes at home, and sometimes both—to dedicate to learning about new technologies. This point underscores the importance of having a supportive manager or supervisor. Because IT and the people who work with it are such large expenses within many organizations, support from the organization's manager is crucial, as described here by Barry, a senior systems analyst:

> Quite often it is easier to get resources allocated in an area of an organization if you have someone at the top at your side. It's really touch and go at mid-level or low-level. People will acknowledge that it's a worthwhile project but at the same time they have their priorities that are outlined from above, and it's tough to get things accomplished. So we would hold meetings and talk about options but when it came to actually, you know, doing any testing or actual work, it's very tough to get anything done.

When insufficient resources are allocated for IT, services, and personnel, this situation can place more burden and stress on those information professionals who remain to do the work. As IT has spread, however, more and more upper-level administrators recognize how critical their organization's information resources are. When they do recognize this, they tend to be more supportive of their information personnel. Just being there to listen to the problems that information personnel have is one way to improve the work situation, as Brenda, an IT and media staff person, said about her upper-level manager:

> I have seen over the years that his door is always open no matter what your position. The door is open and if he is not busy, you just knock and say "Can we talk?" If you want to close the door, he'll say sure, and you can vent as much as you want. He might not be able to do anything to help you, but he will always listen and at some point he may be able to help you immediately. He may not be able to help you for some months or may not be able to help you at all in some cases, but he has at least listened. In some cases I have discovered after many months [that] he has been able to do something to help me with my problem, even

though I perhaps didn't think that he was. I think the [IT] department is very fortunate. I think after 30 years' experience there isn't much he hasn't seen or heard, you know.

As these quotes suggest, support from individuals higher up in the organization is a key element in being able to do an information job successfully. Other people in the organization also have a profound influence on how effective information professionals can be in their organization. As one of our information professionals mentioned in the preceding chapter, many workers in the information field have to deal with end users and their typical resistance to change. Although there is variety in what people like, some workers who use IT and services hate to change: They don't like upgrades, version changes, new products, or even bug fixes. One of our interviewees, Duane, was surprised at the lengths employees would go to in order to try to undermine his efforts:

> People just don't like new stuff. You know, it gets frustrating to implement things when people are actively resisting you. Bringing in new technologies, dealing with people … there is still that gap where people are older and some that are younger. We actually have one (professional) that recently found a typewriter and brought it into his office because he refused to use a computer. And there are some that just want to be hand-held all the time all along the way. Really what I see technology do is enhance their work experience, not impede it. Anyway, they take it as an obstacle rather than a resource.

Not all IT professionals experience this hesitation to embrace new technology among the end users with whom they work. A lot depends upon the type of organization in which one works and the characteristics of the people who make up the end-user community in that company or institution. Organizations that were founded prior to the widespread use of IT and that center around some other well-established profession, such as medicine or the law, often contain employees who resist technological change. Other, younger firms, especially those that have always depended on technology, such as electronics manufacturers and telecommunications companies, may have fewer such employees in their ranks.

Stress, burnout, long hours, a continuous need to keep updated, unsupportive managers, and resistant end users: Many of the quotes included here might lead the reader to believe that this field has enough obstacles that it might be wiser to pursue another profession. Yet a majority of our respondents found their work to be challenging and rewarding, fitting with their temperaments, and well worth the troubles mentioned here. Working in the information professions has a number of advantages, both professionally and in life outside work. For example, one of the professionals we interviewed, Melanie, described how her IT knowledge facilitated her communication with her child:

> Keeping informed and educated on what the technology is and what it can do is important. I have a 15-year-old at home; I would like to know what she is doing. And I don't think if I was not in this field that I would have much knowledge about instant messaging and web surfing and that kind of information. So it keeps me in that loop. Like I said, she knows far more than her brother and sister did just a few short years ago. She is way ahead of what they knew at the same age. So, it keeps me up to date and, "Oh my mom she doesn't know, she doesn't understand," because I do, and she knows it.

In this quote, Melanie describes one of the hidden virtues of being an information professional: Information professionals are often the most up-to-date people in their families and communities with respect to their knowledge of IT and telecommunications. Although not everyone appreciates people asking them questions about web searching, laptops, or home wireless networks, others enjoy being able to help their friends and family with computers and other information-related tasks. In addition to helping others, sometimes knowing a lot about information and technology can also benefit one's own interests and hobbies. Another IT staff person we talked to, Adam, found that he had an interest in creating and producing video that was shared between his work and personal lives:

> I use computers to do things I need to do in my life or want to have fun doing, and I like video ... Video is one of the more resource-intensive computer processes and that really forced me to look at the technology underneath it, and it became a really valuable skill. There are not a lot of people who do [video] around here, and it kind of carved out a niche that I fill in the organization. Because of my interest, I'm able to coordinate a formalized process so that people who want to use it in their jobs can get the help they need.

In the Chapter 10, we refer to a concept called *pervasiveness*, which relates to the fact that many people involved in the information professions have a crossover of interests between their work life and their nonwork life. Adam's quote is a great example of this, and it shows how an interest and skill that Adam developed in his nonwork life was transferable into his profession in a way that gave him a unique and valuable mix of talents for his organization. Although some people who dislike technology find this one of the least attractive parts of some jobs in the information professions, for many people it is a great advantage to be able to take an activity they like to perform on their own time and transfer it into the workplace. Doing so can create a unique niche, as Adam described, and can make a person a very valuable contributor to an organization.

While some professionals bring a skill from home into the workplace, others bring skills from work into their nonwork life. James, an information professional we interviewed, described a situation in which, after work, he still performs many IT-related tasks:

I think that sometimes I do more IT work outside of work than inside at work. And I spend eight hours here. I think that there are always the friends that you have that will always be calling saying, "Oops, I did something to my computer, how do I make this work right?" And the perception is that the IT guy knows how to do everything, of course. But at the same time I think that everyone in this field loves to learn what they do not know about computers, and we have enough of a familiarity with how things work that we can actually roll up our sleeves, dive in, and actually look like we know what we are doing.

Although James did not say so in his quote, other professionals we interviewed mentioned that they received a kind of social prestige from being able to help friends and family members with their technology problems. Some reported that they had been treated to many free dinners after being invited to people's houses to socialize and, oh by the way, I've been having this little problem with my laptop.

Another advantage to working in the information professions is that the constant changes that occur also ensure variety from year to year in a person's job. Especially in the environment of a smaller company, an information professional often gets a chance to exercise a wide range of skills on a variety of interesting tasks. Many of the managers of information professionals recognize and appreciate their flexibility, and this helps to give information professionals a sense of satisfaction. Clint, whom we also previously quoted, had this to say:

You sort of need to be a jack of all trades. You have to be aware of a lot of things that perhaps a purchasing agent would be aware of. You have to know that there are certain clauses written into your contracts. You have to know to be able to check those, you have to keep lists. There is a lot of upfront thinking that goes into negotiating, more than anyone would ever believe, and my boss [an IT director] spends an awful lot of his time doing this with me. You sort of have to be a little bit buyer, a little bit of a lawyer. I find that I need to know a little about a lot of things.

In addition to encouraging a high degree of flexibility, working in the information professions brings a person into contact with an enormous diversity of different people, particularly if serving in a role that has a lot of contact with end users. Having a sense of humor is a bonus. Ellen, a database manager and general computing teacher, reported the following funny story to show some of the things she enjoys about her job:

> Last year, the very first class, I had 16 students. One lady that was from Ukraine, she had 7 children, she raised her children, and she was in her late 40s, and this was one of the very first times that her husband had let her out of the house. She spoke very little English ... I am talking to them, showing them, you know, this is a monitor, this is a keyboard, and I go, "This is the mouse." She screamed! Jumped on her chair and screamed, "Mouse, mouse!" But you know, so I took a step backward and lifted it up, and I showed it to her, and I said, "Mouse, mouse."

Those who are successful in the information professions often exhibit a great deal of what researchers call *affective commitment.* This emotional attachment they have to their work reflects their eagerness to stay in their profession. The vast majority of our professional interviewees clearly showed us a lasting enjoyment for the diversity of their work, the challenges of their organizations, and most important, the crucial role they play in their jobs. Contemporary organizations recognize this importance more and more, and they implement strategies to retain and recruit qualified information professionals.

In closing this chapter, we feel we would be remiss if we did not acknowledge that there are too few individuals from underrepresented minorities and too few women occupying jobs in the information professions. When we asked Adam, whom we previously quoted, if women played a substantial role in the departments where he had worked, he provided the following comments:

> Good question, unfortunately no, if I look at the broad picture, unfortunately no. I look at my own [experience], the answer is yes. In my previous position actually I worked in a department where the IT manager and IT director were both women, which is very unusual in my experience, but I actually worked for a boss who had come out of 19 years of IT experience in the industry with a degree in computer science and programming, which is also not traditionally thought of as a female career path. Also in that same IT department, the majority of the IT staff were women. I don't know if that was impacted because I was working in the school district or not, but I will say that it was refreshing to see the change, women being interested in IT.

Lack of diversity in some areas of the information workplace is a consequence of relatively few young women and young people from underrepresented minorities interested in pursuing IT related majors and careers. In Chapter 10, we examine in detail a few of the key reasons the information workplace has sometimes been seen as unwelcoming to women and underrepresented minorities. Finally, in the closing section of the book, we examine the educational component of this problem and what we can all do to improve the level of diversity in the information professions.

References

McMurtrey, M. E., Grover, V., Teng, J. T. C., & Lightner, N. J. (2002). Job satisfaction of information technology workers: The impact of career orientation and task automation in a CASE environment. *Journal of Management Information Systems, 19*(2), 273–302.

Moore, J. E. (2000). One road to turnover: An examination of work exhaustion in technology professionals. *MIS Quarterly, 24*(1), 141–168.

Niederman, F., & Moore, J. E. (2000). *Computer personnel research: What have we learned in this decade?* Paper presented at the Special Interest Group on Computer Personnel Research Annual Conference, Chicago, IL.

Sadler, P. (1994). Gold collar workers: What makes them play at their best? *Personnel Management* (April), 14–17.

CHAPTER 10

Stereotypes, Culture, and the Information Professions

A young cousin of mine taking a computer course was really upset that the professor had shown this highly acclaimed video, Triumph of the Nerds. *It leaves out any role women have ever had in computing … The women in this class get the message that they have to be different or strange to get into this field.*

—Anita Borg, PhD,
award-winning computer scientist

Aleks Krotoski was identified in 2006 as No. 9 on the top 10 list of "girl geeks" by CNET.UK,[1] just above Paris Hilton (well-known for her interests in computer gaming) and just below Marie Curie (the late scientist and two-time Nobel prize winner). In the same year, Krotoski was named as one of the top 100 most influential women in the computer gaming industry. Krotoski's career defies easy categorization: She is a writer, a researcher, a doctoral student, a computer gamer, an entrepreneur, and a public policy advocate. She earned a bachelor's and a master's degree in psychology, but she is most influential in an industry that has long been considered highly technological and male dominated.

When prompted to think about what kind of person makes a career in information technology (IT), people commonly respond with a stereotyped description: a somewhat antisocial individual who prefers machines to people and who lacks varied interests outside of building computer hardware or writing software. In U.S. society, it is common for individuals who work with technology to be tagged as a geek, nerd, or another similar label. However, as Krotoski shows, a so-called girl geek can in reality be a sociable and influential person with a wide range of interests and talents. In this light, being a geek is something to be proud of, something that signifies a high level of expertise and knowledge in an area that many people care deeply about such as computer gaming.

But the idea that geeks are respected and respectable is a relatively new one. There are many places in school or at work where being labeled as a geek is still meant to be an insult. People who work in the more technical areas of the information field have gotten used to this, so much so that it is one of several cultural characteristics of being in the information field. For newcomers to the information professions, it can be important to be aware of these cultural characteristics because they affect the atmosphere in many workplace settings. By knowing in advance what the workplace will be like, newcomers can be prepared to deal with the challenges they may encounter there. Understanding these issues can also allow managers who work with information professionals to develop better ways of improving the adjustment, attitudes, and retention of employees.

Culture is an idea that is widely used to describe people who live in different regions of the world (Hall, 1959, 1976). For example, think of how the phrases *European culture* or *Californian culture* remind us of how people from these different areas of the world think and act. Culture is also used to describe particular workplaces; *organizational culture* refers to the typical ways that people think and act in companies, government agencies, and educational institutions (Hofstede & Hofstede, 2005).

Occupational culture, which is yet a third way of thinking about culture, refers to shared ways of thinking and acting among individuals who work in particular careers (Trice, 1993; Trice & Beyer, 1984, 1993). Occupational cultures have their own unique characteristics that people learn through their educational experiences and through working with others who do similar jobs. Many people see their work not just as a paycheck but also as a place to develop friendships and as a source of satisfaction and emotional support (Trice & Beyer, 1993). The mastery of tasks in a particular occupation becomes a part of a person's self-concept. When people meet, the first question they may ask each other is, What do you do? In response, a person may answer, "I'm a librarian" or "I'm a web developer." Many people draw part of their personal identities from their occupations.

Information professionals have their own occupational cultures— shared ways of thinking and acting that are common to many others in their field—even though they may work in many different organizational settings. An informal way of thinking about this is to imagine that people in an occupation have a kind of "club" that they belong to that sets them apart from people in other types of jobs. Information professionals have clubs that set them apart from doctors, politicians, and auto mechanics. Many of the jobs in the information professions have cultural similarities to one another, although there are also important differences among them, depending upon the particular job. For instance, help-desk worker and systems administrator are both IT jobs, but help-desk workers interact directly with end users every day, while systems administrators generally do not. As a result, occupations are more of a stew than a broth: They usually have many subspecialties, each with its own unique subculture.

These subcultures evolve as new technologies, innovations, and discoveries drive the development of new occupations. At present, job titles among information professionals are diverse, numerous, and changing because of the many different situations in which IT is used, the many different types of hardware and software that are emerging, and the variety of data that exist (e.g., health data, maps, financial information, climate data, and so on). Jobs such as information manager, system librarian, and database security specialist didn't exist in any great numbers just a few years ago, but they are becoming increasingly common today.

One way to tell when an occupation has become mature and mainstream is to look at the professional associations that arise to organize and assist people who work in a given area. Within the information field, the Association for Computing Machinery (ACM) is one national association that has helped to develop undergraduate curricula for commonly offered majors such as computer science, information systems, and IT. Another is the American Society for Information Science and Technology (ASIST), which serves information professionals with backgrounds in a diverse range of areas, such as computer science, linguistics, management, librarianship, engineering, and education. ACM, founded in 1947, is "a major force in advancing the skills of information technology professionals and students worldwide." Founded in 1937, ASIST has the mission of "leading the search for new and better theories, techniques, and technologies to improve access to information."

Once an occupation is well established, entry into the occupation by newcomers begins to follow a common process: attraction, access, adjustment, identification, and commitment. Figure 10.1 shows the process of occupational socialization. A person must know about an occupation and feel an *attraction* toward some aspect of it. For instance, the relatively obscure occupation of criminal forensics grew rapidly some years ago, partly because a popular television show depicted the field as glamorous and exciting. As individuals become aware of educational or job opportunities, they take advantage of options they see as attractive, and they gradually become more involved in the occupation. In the field of IT, many examples exist of tinkerers who experimented with computers and software in a garage or basement before deciding to pursue education or a career in a technology-related area.

Various factors affect whether a person has *access* to and can successfully enter an occupation (Trice, 1993; Trice & Beyer, 1984, 1993). A family's socioeconomic status influences a child's knowledge about and aspirations for a given occupation. Kids learn from their parents,

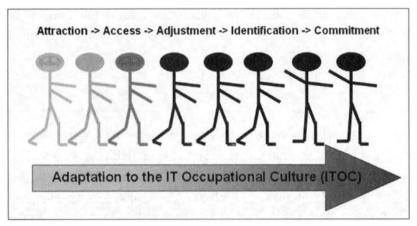

Figure 10.1 The process of occupational socialization

peers, and teachers about which jobs may be available to them. As already noted, the popular media also influence kids' beliefs about the occupations available to them. In the 1930s and 1940s, hundreds of dramatic paperbacks about nursing were published and marketed as a reflection of the widespread cultural assumption that nursing was one of the few professional careers available to women.

As individuals become acquainted with an occupation, they decide whether they can fit within that occupation. In other words, do they have the intellectual and emotional capabilities to carry out its activities? Are they willing to conform to the rules of behavior for that occupation? Does their personal temperament enable them to deal with the demands of the occupation's pattern of activities? This process is known as *adjustment*, and like the aspiring medical student who fainted at the sight of blood, some people learn that the activities and working conditions of an occupation are not suitable for them.

As entry into the occupation continues, the time commitment involved in advancing in a career limits individuals' ability to branch out into other occupations. Professional involvement with other people in the occupation and respect from professionals in other occupations reinforces a sense of *identification* with the occupation.

Individuals identify socially and psychologically with the occupation, and when asked "What do you do?" they respond with the name of their occupation: "I'm an engineer" or "I'm a librarian."

People who spend many years in a career path tend to become more and more *committed* to their occupation. They accumulate seniority benefits from being in the occupation that they would lose if they left it. They develop loyalties to other members of the occupation and to professional groups. They develop habits of thought and behavior common to people in that occupation. Commitment can take many forms: a sense of emotional attachment to the occupation ("I love this work"), a belief that loyalty or persistence is considered desirable in the occupation ("Everyone knows you have to stick with it if you want to get ahead in this work"), or a belief in a lack of alternatives ("There's no other work I could do that would pay so well"). Professional associations play an important role in promoting the identification with and commitment to occupations. They provide an established reference group of other professionals as well as organized political influence at a state or national level. Professional associations also give members support and protection by specifying the proper modes of behavior. For example, the American Library Association advocates on behalf of librarians who are asked to censor books. In Appendix D of this book, we include links to some websites of associations related to the information professions along with excerpts from their codes of ethics.

During our research for writing this book, we asked information professionals how they became involved in their work; in other words, what were their processes of attraction, access, adjustment, identification, and commitment? We conducted and analyzed 56 interviews, nine focus groups, and 215 surveys over five years of our research with experienced information professionals as well as among students who were training for jobs in the information field (Guzman, Sharif, Kwiatkowska, & Li, 2006; Guzman, 2005, 2008a, 2008b; Guzman, Sharif, Blanchard, Ellis, & Stanton, 2005). We were particularly interested in how information jobs have been changing over time and how these changes have affected the advancement of women and underrepresented minorities in the information professions.

We found that those people who developed positive perceptions of the occupational culture early in their education become more committed to it. People with hands-on experience in the information field reported more positive perceptions of the profession. Educational experiences that realistically simulated work activities helped students to become more comfortable with its occupational culture; this includes internships and co-op work experiences (getting course credit while working part-time during the regular academic semester). Gaining work experience also increased the confidence that students have in meeting the demands of their occupations and enjoyment of facing the challenges.

Our interview and survey results showed that working information professionals especially enjoyed lifelong learning by getting involved in activities that allow them to acquire more knowledge and skills (especially skills with the latest and most novel technologies). Some of the most popular ways of acquiring knowledge involve what people often refer to as "playing with technology," or experimenting with and testing new technologies through hands-on activities. Another popular method was taking certification courses that provide a focused sense of accomplishment with one particular brand or type of technology (e.g., the Linux operating system). Additionally, people enjoy learning collaboratively through interacting with each other online in environments such as wikis and open source software projects.

Another feature of the occupational culture that mattered to a person's level of commitment is a characteristic we call *pervasiveness*. The idea of pervasiveness relates to the degree to which a person integrates technology into daily life and leisure activities. We found that people who enjoyed using technology outside of work also enjoyed its being part of their occupation. Individuals who were comfortable using information technologies, such as cell phones, digital cameras, GPS devices, online games, and so on in everyday life, also felt more comfortable using technology extensively in the context of the workplace.

Our complete portrait of early career information professionals thus emerged as people with a positive outlook toward technology, an enjoyment of hands-on technology activities, an attitude of life-long learning, an appreciation of the latest cutting-edge technology, and a pervasive integration of technology into their daily lives.

Now think back to the beginning of this chapter: This description seems to fit Aleks Krotoski, No. 9 girl geek in the world. In the first phase of our research, 23 out of 27 participants mentioned geek and nerd as the stereotypes or labels they have heard applied to people in the information professions. The geek label has become mainstream; popular websites such Asgeek.com, ThinkGeek.com, Innergeek.us, GeekCode.com, MajorGeeks.com, and Geekgirls.com provide information and resources for geeks. A variety of books, such as *The Geeks' Guide to World Domination: Be Afraid, Beautiful People,* and *Geek Chic: The Ultimate Guide to Geek Culture,* celebrate the value and importance of geeks within society. A short-lived 2005 TV game show called *Beauty and the Geek* paired male geeks with female models, while the *Revenge of the Nerds* franchise spun off movies and television shows for nearly a decade.

Despite this exposure in popular culture, the label of geek or nerd is still accompanied by some negative stereotypes, such as the idea that such people lack social skills. In our research, we found that many newcomers in the information professions do not like being stigmatized as nerds or geeks. Does this influence the choices of students with respect to majoring in IT or related fields? If people who are already part of the workforce have difficulties accepting these labels when applied to themselves, we hypothesized that individuals in the process of entering the field might feel even more strongly about this.

In our research, white students tended to report fewer concerns about being stereotyped as a geek or nerd than members of underrepresented minority groups. In an earlier study, Igbaria and Wormley (1992) also looked at race differences in career success of information systems professionals. They noted that minorities had found it more challenging to advance professionally and managerially within their organizations: "Minorities may experience considerable discrimination on their jobs, which lowers their performance and ultimately impedes their career advancement" (Igbaria & Wormley, 1992, p. 507). If minority members already perceive lack of social acceptance due to race or ethnicity, adding the derogatory label of geek or nerd might make the occupation less attractive.

In addition, our research indicated that white students reported a higher average level of enjoyment associated with keeping up with the latest technology than did minority students, a difference on what we called the *esoteric knowledge scale*. Likewise, in the interviews and focus groups we conducted, minority students suggested that they sometimes had less access to technology for personal experimentation. This lack could be attributed to circumstances within their families, schools, or communities that limited early opportunities for hands-on experiences with technology.

Finally, our results showed that males reported higher self-efficacy or confidence dealing with technology challenges than did females. This finding was consistent with previous studies that found that females have significantly lower self-efficacy than male students regarding traditionally male-dominated subjects, including computer science (Busch, 1995).

We highlight these findings not to discourage women and members of underrepresented minorities from pursuing a career in the information professions but rather to prepare them for the idea that there will be challenges and barriers to overcome. Undoubtedly in the future, we will look back and marvel that these barriers existed, much as we marvel today that years ago many people believed that women could not succeed as doctors, lawyers, or diplomats. But for now, it is important to be prepared for the idea that one may be called geek or nerd as an insult. For now, in some schools and workplaces, information professionals will not get the respect they deserve. But several minority students and professionals from our research indicated that they simply shrugged off the geek label because they "loved communicating with other people," and they did not fit any-one's stereotype of a geek or nerd. We see this positive attitude as a beginning indication that information professionals will soon take control over the image of their profession. As IT becomes more and more central to the functioning of society, with cell phones, GPS technology, virtual worlds, and a hundred other technologies as yet unseen, the importance of the information professional's role seems likely to become better respected.

Meanwhile, in Table 10.1, we've summarized what it means to be an information geek—and we mean that in most positive possible sense. Note that these characteristics apply to the jobs and settings where working with technology is a primary feature of the role. For example, these jobs would include systems administrator or network engineer. Other roles and positions with a lesser emphasis on technology, such as digital librarian or project manager, were not discussed as thoroughly by our participants, so it is likely that some of the features described in Table 10.1 would not apply to those jobs.

Table 10.1   Features of Information Technology Occupational Culture

Occupational Feature	Description
Value of IT Knowledge	Members of the occupation value IT expertise and technical skills; technical knowledge and skills are essential for providing effective information systems to organizations.
Use of Jargon	The proliferation of new products and services leads to a wide array of acronyms, brand names, and specialized terminology; understanding and use of this terminology creates professional and social divisions between IT people and non-IT people.
IT Pervasiveness	Many members of the occupation integrate technology into non-work leisure time and socializing. For instance, many IT people continue developing their IT skills at home or may have friends that are also IT people.
Geek/Nerd Social Stigma	Members of the occupation are frequently stigmatized by nonmembers as nerds or geeks or by other negative labels. Members share an awareness of this negative stigmatization and use different strategies to manage it (e.g., acceptance).
Enjoyment of IT Challenges	The occupation offers many challenges such as the rapid development of new technology and the consequent need for continued updating of technical knowledge and skills. Some roles require long or unusual hours.
IT as a Helping Profession	Many professional roles in the occupation involve helping people with solving IT problems small and large. IT people also help their friends and relatives with their home computers.

As you review the features of the occupation described in Table 10.1, consider whether each characteristic sounds positive or not and whether each one is something you might use to describe yourself. If you can see yourself in some or all of these descriptions, you would probably have little difficulty fitting into the occupational culture that you would find among other students in your field of study or other co-workers in your area.

In the next section of the book, we will expand on the features of the information professions and examine the educational options and strategies that students can explore to make a career in information. Pursuing a successful career in the information professions requires an awareness of the features of the profession, as well as thorough preparation in the fundamentals of information and technology. Numerous educational options exist for this preparation, and we will discuss many of them in the chapters that follow.

Endnotes

1. Accessed on September 20, 2009 at crave.cnet.co.uk/gadgets/0,39029552, 49285435,00.htm.

References

Busch, T. (1995). Gender differences in self-efficacy and attitudes toward computers. *Journal of Educational Computing Research, 12,* 147–158.

Guzman, I., Sharif, R., Kwiatkowska, A., & Li, Q. (2006). *Occupational culture and commitment in the IT profession: A multi-country perspective.* Paper presented at the 2006 Americas Conference on Information Systems, Acapulco, Mexico.

Guzman, I. R. (2005). *As you like IT: The occupational acculturation of information technologists.* Paper presented at Connections 2005: The 10th Great Lakes Information Science Conference, Montreal, QC, Canada.

Guzman, I. R. (2008a). *As you like IT. Culture and commitment of new IT people: Using mixed methodology to study the perceptions of new information technologists.* Saarbrücken, Germany: VDM Verlag.

Guzman, I. R. (2008b). Occupational culture and socialization in information systems. In T. Torres & M. Arias (Eds.), *Encyclopedia of HRIS: Challenges in e-HRM.* Pittsburgh, PA: Idea Group.

Guzman, I. R., Sharif, R. M., Blanchard, T. J., Ellis, G. S., & Stanton, J. M. (2005). *What attracts women to the IT field? The first process of occupational socialization.* Paper presented at the 2005 Americas Conference on Information Systems, Omaha, NE.

Hall, E. T. (1959). *The silent language.* Garden City, NY: Doubleday.

Hall, E. T. (1976). *Beyond culture.* Garden City, NY: Anchor Press.

Hofstede, G., & Hofstede, G. J. (2005). *Cultures and organizations: Software of the mind: Intercultural cooperation and its importance for survival.* New York: McGraw Hill.

Igbaria, M., & Wormley, W. (1992). Organizational experiences and career success of MIS professionals and managers: An examination of race differences. *MIS Quarterly, 16*(4), 507–529.

Trice, H. M. (1993). *Occupational subcultures in the workplace.* Ithaca, NY: ILR Press.

Trice, H. M., & Beyer, J. M. (1984). Studying organizational cultures through rites and ceremonials. *Academy of Management Review, 9*(4), 653.

Trice, H. M., & Beyer, J. M. (1993). *The cultures of work organizations.* Englewood Cliffs, NJ: Prentice Hall.

PART 3

What's Next?

The chapters in the final section provide some perspective on the future of the information professions and how students can prepare for that future. In Chapter 11, we describe the background behind a new bit of jargon: *Cyberinfrastructure* refers to a vision of information as a substrate for society that supports every aspect of what we do—education, government, business, research, transportation, defense, and so forth. Chapter 12 brings a contemporary perspective to the profession of librarianship and shows how this longstanding profession fits in with other aspects of the information field. Continuing in this same vein, Chapter 13 explains how some schools have begun to integrate the education of librarians and other information professionals into a novel interdisciplinary mixture. Chapter 14 describes some of the background behind the difficulties that some educational programs have experienced with diversity, recruitment, and retention of women and students of color. Finally, Chapter 15 looks to the future of the information professions with advice for students about how to prepare for and get a good education that integrates the knowledge of information and technology.

CHAPTER 11

Cyberinfrastructure:
A Long Word for the Future
of Information Technology

*Ensuring that the U.S. continues to lead the world in
science and technology will be a central priority for
my administration.*
　　　　　—Barack Obama, President of the United States

Dan Atkins is one smart guy. After earning a combined PhD in elec-
trical engineering and computer science from the University of
Illinois, he proceeded to the University of Michigan, where he
became a tenured professor, then associate dean of the engineering
school, then interim dean of the school, and finally founding dean of
Michigan's School of Information.[1] (We will have more to say about
schools of information in Chapter 13.) He also won two distinguished service awards from his university plus the Nina W.
Mathesson Award for outstanding contributions to medical informatics, a *Computerworld* Smithsonian Award, and the Paul Evan Peters
Award for internationally recognized achievements related to computer networking. Perhaps the most singular achievement in a singu-
larly distinguished career, however, was Atkins' 2003 publication of
the "Report of the National Science Foundation Blue-Ribbon Advisory
Panel on Cyberinfrastructure." Actually, Atkins was the first author
among nine highly distinguished contributors from universities and

industry, but not unexpectedly, the report is often referred to as the *Atkins Report* because of his lead role.

Before we begin examining the report, we should take a moment to peel back the layers of the word *cyberinfrastructure*. Whoever chose this 19-letter mouthful must have had a fun day poking through the dictionary desperately seeking just the right word, but the result is a bit unwieldy and abstract. It also inadvertently overemphasizes the hardware aspects of information technology. The blue ribbon report defines it in the following way:

> The term infrastructure has been used since the 1920s to refer collectively to the roads, power grids, telephone systems, bridges, rail lines, and similar public works that are required for an industrial economy to function. Although good infrastructure is often taken for granted and noticed only when it stops functioning, it is among the most complex and expensive thing that society creates. The newer term cyberinfrastructure refers to infrastructure based upon distributed computer, information and communication technology. If infrastructure is required for an industrial economy, then we could say that cyberinfrastructure is required for a knowledge economy. (Atkins et al., 2003, p. 5)

Yet just a few pages later, the report discusses a much more expansive view of cyberinfrastructure that includes intangible elements such as social practices, personnel, and institutions. The authors realized that the technology by itself is just a bunch of boxes with blinking lights and that you have to put software, standards, policies, and people into the mix to have something truly useful. Thus, in practice the word cyberinfrastructure has become a vague way to refer to almost anything related to the use of high-speed networking technology and the extensive collections of computers and other gadgets connected by those networks. More important, while the report focused on the uses and usefulness of cyberinfrastructure for science (think physics, biology, and astronomy) and engineering (think bridges, computers, and space shuttles), the use of the term has now extended into the social sciences, such as psychology, as well as into government, business, and other areas. So what began as a fancy new term for fancy network hardware has now become a catchall word for a whole pile of interconnected concepts having to do with modern networked information technology. We like the following somewhat modified version of a definition provided by the Research Computing division of University Information Technology Services at Indiana University:

> Cyberinfrastructure consists of computing systems, data storage systems, advanced instruments and data reposito-ries, visualization environments, and people, all linked together by software and high performance networks to improve [research] productivity and enable breakthroughs not otherwise possible.[2]

In this quote, we have intentionally placed the term *research* in brackets to reflect our belief that cyberinfrastructure actually has the potential to improve productivity and enable breakthroughs in a vari-ety of areas in addition to scientific research, such as business, gov-ernment, nonprofits, and others. In fact, as the original definition suggested, cyberinfrastructure has woven itself into the quilt of American life as the underlying support structure for our beloved cel-lular phones, credit cards, cable television channels, YouTube videos, and pretty much everything else that transmits, stores, or processes information in any form.

Now back to the blue ribbon report. Atkins and his colleagues had the benefit of a bird's-eye view of the National Science Foundation (NSF), a federal agency established in 1950 to shepherd and support scientific research in all areas except health and medicine (research in these areas is supported by the National Institutes of Health). The NSF has a long history of funding key developments in the informa-tion fields, most notably many of the fundamental technological ingredients of the internet, of search engines such as Google, and of key repositories of scientific information such as the National Science Digital Library. (NSF funds other cool stuff too, such as Antarctic exploration, brain research, and nanotechnology.) With the insider's view of these many previously funded technology projects, Atkins and his colleagues made some provocative guesses about where cyberinfrastructure was headed. And with the benefit of several years' intervening experience since the report was published, many of those guesses look prophetic.

In order to understand those predictions, we have to get a bit more detailed view of what cyberinfrastructure is. Using the report as a guide, we've taken the essential building blocks of cyberinfrastructure and made a little schematic in Table 11.1. The schematic shows a layer cake of technology with the most essential forms of equipment at the bottom and the people at the top.

Table 11.1   Schematic Representation of Cyberinfrastructure

V	Individual Users	Groups/Networks	Institutions
IV	Analysis Tools	Search/Q&A Tools	Social Tools
	Visualization Tools	Curation Tools	Communication Tools
III	Middleware		
II	Computational Grids	Storage Grids	Sensor Arrays
I	High-Speed Networks		

On the bottom layer, labeled with Roman numeral I, is the key ingredient that makes cyberinfrastructure possible, the high-speed network. Many people in the U.S. have broadband internet connections at work and at home. Others still have, or can remember, dial-up connections to the internet. Roughly speaking, a broadband internet connection transmits data about 10 times faster than dial-up, a great improvement that makes possible a range of new web services such as TV-quality streaming video. In comparison, the Internet2 consortium, which has been working on innovations to improve the internet, has created a demonstration network called

Abilene, which moves data 180,000 times faster than dial-up. At these speeds, the contents of an entire DVD containing a two-hour movie, special features, director's commentary, and all the other features on the disk could be transferred from one location in the world to another location in a matter of seconds. What new products and services might be possible if every business in the U.S. could send and receive information at those speeds?

At Layer II, we have the various arrays of devices that are interconnected by the high-speed networks of Layer I. A grid is a group of computers or other electronic devices that can work as a coordinated team. This teamwork makes it possible to divide larger problems into smaller pieces and then hand out the small pieces to members of the team. One of the first groups to try this was the Space Sciences Laboratory at the University of California, Berkeley. The lab was continuously collecting radio signals from the Arecibo radio telescope in Puerto Rico, looking for signs of intelligent life on other planets. The problem was that there was way too much recorded signal data to be processed by any one computer, even a supercomputer. So the lab's research team created software that divided the recorded radio signals into various chunks and sent each chunk out for analysis to a home computer that was sitting idle while the owner was making dinner. Although the Space Sciences Laboratory has not (yet) found any signs of intelligent life on other worlds, it did demonstrate very neatly the potential of grid computing to address difficult analysis problems. The same idea has been applied to data storage and access, with the result that one may now store a single piece of information in multiple locations (for the sake of safety and speed of access) without ever getting confused about whether the copy you happen to get is up to date. This would be equivalent to stashing some of your money in one pair of pants and then automatically having that money available in any other pair of pants you own. Some of the massive amounts of information stored and analyzed by these grids come from sensors attached to the internet. One example of a limited kind of public sensor network is the thousands of webcams that provide live images from all around the world. Internet-connected sensors also track weather, air pollution, urban traffic, and the stock market. With enough sensors of different types, along with storage to archive the results, and computational power to analyze all of the data, these Layer II machines comprise a powerful set of building blocks for new ways that people can learn, work, and play.

To tie these building blocks together, we have the middleware that comprises Layer III. *Middleware* is another one of those vague catchall terms, but it generally refers to computer software that is invisible to most of us because it works among systems rather than between systems and people. Anytime you have a complicated set of computers, sensors, or other gizmos and you want them to work together, there has to be software "glue" that sticks them together. That glue ensures that the different machines stay coordinated with each other and that they can communicate among themselves. Middleware also helps to maintain security and privacy by keeping track of who is who and who owns what. In Chapter 4, we discussed how technology development has become easier and that many software creation tasks can now be accomplished by individuals who are not experts. Middleware is one of the exceptions to that rule: Middleware developers must have a thorough knowledge of all of the systems that have to be glued together, all of the protocols (languages that systems use to communicate with one another), and the overall architecture of the system that that they are trying to build out of all of the component parts.

At Layer IV, we have the tools with which we can directly interact as computer users. Most people who have worked with computers are familiar with the most basic application tools: productivity applications such as spreadsheets and word processors that comprise the essential ingredients of any personal computer. However, the kinds of tools that cyberinfrastructure can provide transcend these basic applications by providing much greater power and interconnectedness. Taking a few familiar examples first, consider the communication tools provided by Skype. Videoconferencing, teleconferencing, text chat, and other abilities all roll together into one polished product, which, for many purposes, people can use for free to stay in touch with each other. Likewise, social networking tools such as LinkedIn, Facebook, and MySpace allow people to stay in touch by forming and maintaining a circle of close contacts. Finally, search, which comes in familiar packages such as Yahoo!, MSN, and Google, provides a way of finding who is out there and what information they have made available to the rest of us. Web search is one example of a bigger concept called information retrieval. Making information retrieval better and making it work for all kinds of data (not just text) is one of the most pressing research problems in cyberinfrastructure. If you have ever tried to search for the blog of your friend John Smith (or anyone else with a common name), you understand the need for better information retrieval tools.

Newer and less familiar capabilities arise from analysis, visualization, and curation tools. For years, statistical and spreadsheet programs have provided the ability to create graphs of various types, but these methods are inconvenient, hard to use for large amounts of data, and generally work well only for numeric data such as measurements and counts. Newer visualization tools work with text (e.g., extracted from webpages), geographical data, sensor data, and information from the operation of the internet itself. A fun example of such new visualization tools is the word mapping program available at Wordle (www.wordle.net), which produces a mosaic of words with their font sizes proportional to the frequency of usage in the source text. Figure 11.1 shows a Wordle visualization[3] based on input from the blog of information security expert Bruce Schneier, an author and researcher who specializes in understanding the origins and outcomes of attacks on information systems. As the visualization suggests, his blog has recently focused on various types of internet scams and how those scams take advantage of their victims.

Analysis goes hand-in-hand with visualization to provide input into decision making for managers, government officials, and researchers. Statistical applications such as SAS and SPSS have provided analysis tools for numeric data for years. More recently, packages such as Atlas.ti and NVivo have provided capabilities for analyzing textual data. Since 2002, the Max Planck Institute for

Figure 11.1   Word visualization of Bruce Schneier's blog

Psycholinguistics in the Netherlands has been developing and improving a software package called ELAN for annotating and analyzing audio and video streams. Although ELAN and similar packages do not provide the level of convenience and power that numeric statistical programs now provide, it is not improbable that in the near future, tools will become available that contain such automation. Imagine a setup where you would type in the website address where terrorists or fanatics are posting videos and commenting on them. Your systems then proceed to vacuum up the video, audio, and text in the all of the pages at that site, convert and translate that mass of data into structured text presented in your native language, and then analyze all that text to uncover trends and predictions about the beliefs and behaviors of the people in question. Cyberinfrastructure makes this possible because the tools in Layer IV are running on top of middleware that connects you to so much of the underlying storage, processing, and other devices needed to perform such analysis.

This brings us to the topmost layer, Layer V, the people layer. It does sound funny to think of people as cyberinfrastructure, but keep in mind that we are not talking about individual human beings such as you or the three authors of this book but rather about the roles and activities of small, medium, or large groups of people. The introduction of the personal computer in the 1980s and the rise in popularity of laptops, notebooks, and netbooks over recent years tend to make us think about computers as personal productivity tools. But the real power of cyberinfrastructure comes from tying us all together into groups, organizations, institutions, and even larger aggregations such as societies. For example, there has been unrest in Iran surrounding presidential election results. Despite efforts by the Iranian government to prevent people from reaching out to the rest of the world (particularly using the internet), lots of information has been leaking out of the country ("Iran's Nonrepublic," 2009). People loyal to the opposition candidate have used cell phone pictures, videos, and text messages to document protests, and they have used Twitter, YouTube, Facebook, and other social networking tools to coordinate and communicate with their followers. Thirty years ago, such groups would have likely only had the traditional landline telephone system available for communication and coordination; monopoly governance of most telephone networks (e.g., by a national phone service or a single telephone company) made it relatively easy for governments to monitor and control the flow of information. However, with cyberinfrastructure, political parties, opposition groups, citizen watchdogs, and others have a flexible, reliable, and diverse set of communication and coordination networks available to them. In some senses, the social and communication tools made possible by cyberinfrastructure facilitate the creation of novel forms of human organization and activity at Layer V that were previously difficult or impossible to achieve.

Here's another great example of cyberinfrastructure at work. If you visit Gapminder (www.gapminder.org), you will find an interactive web application that creates graphs. These graphs are not the ordinary kind of graphs you might find in a newspaper, however. These graphs display animations that chart the movement of various indicators over time. The graphing application is built on top of a massive database that contains data from hundreds of countries around the world and dozens of key indicators collected by governments, nongovernmental agencies, nonprofits, and economic development agencies. The application is free for everyone to use, does not require a download or installation onto your computer, and loads into a web browser in a few seconds. The application can display a comprehensive picture of two or three variables and show their progress over recent years or, in some cases, all the way back to the 1800s. For example, in two clicks, we selected the literacy rate for adult females (percent of females ages 15 and above able to write a short sentence about themselves in their native language) and the gross domestic product (GDP) per employee (in inflation-adjusted 1990 U.S. dollars). Figure 11.2 shows the results.[4]

We highlighted two countries that showed different patterns between 1992 and 1999, namely Saudi Arabia and Portugal. Each of the progressions appears in Figure 11.2 with a corresponding label, Saudi Arabia to the left and Portugal to the right. The line of bubbles next to each label shows the progression over time. The bubbles for Saudi Arabia are slightly larger, reflecting a somewhat larger overall population. Both countries show progress over time in female literacy, Saudi Arabia from about 56 percent to almost 70 percent and Portugal from 85 percent up to about 90 percent. However, productivity shows

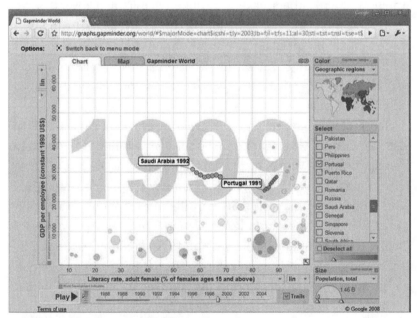

Figure 11.2   Example of Gapminder graph

a gradual decline in Saudi Arabia between 1991 and 1999, while in Portugal it shows a steep rise. We leave it to the reader to interpret these results. The important point with respect to this chapter is the simplicity, ease, and power of accessing a universe of statistics about our planet and its people. Making this possible required all of the elements of cyberinfrastructure that we described above.

But Gapminder could be much better. Most of the data only goes up to 2006 or so. What if the data could go all the way up to the present, or better yet, be updated in real time? Also, even though there are many indicators—or variables—to work with, a lot of the variables you might want to examine are not available. Gapminder does not have information about college graduation rates, or gasoline consumption, or out-of-pocket healthcare costs, or any of a hundred other variables that researchers, students, policy makers, and others might like to see. So there is still room for improvement. And on that note, let's return to the Atkins Report and see what the expectations are for cyberinfrastructure.

The report describes future trends and implications for 14 areas of science and engineering. We have taken the liberty of organizing these into a smaller set of topics and translating the implications into areas of public concern: the environment, health, industry, and the economy. With respect to the environment, the most important implication of cyberinfrastructure by far is the improved ability of scientists, researchers, and governments to understand our changing climate. Although opinions vary on the long-term impacts of global warming, there are few remaining doubters who claim that our environment is not changing as a result of human use of fossil fuels, decreases and changes to forest lands, and increases in intensive agriculture. Cyberinfrastructure is leading to an international network of sensors, databases, modeling and visualization tools, and collaborative networks of researchers whose capability for understanding and predicting changes to the environment are improving at a colossal rate.

In the area of health, cyberinfrastructure has greased the wheels of progress in bioinformatics as biologists and medical researchers have documented and probed the genetic structure of our species and many others. In the near future, we can expect substantial progress in the new area of proteomics, the scientific understanding of how genetic structure regulates the creation of proteins in living creatures. For example, the report describes the problem of visualizing protein folding (i.e., being able to predict how a particular biological molecule changes its shape as it is formed and as it is affected by other molecular structures). Researchers in drug companies, cancer centers, and universities are making ever-increasing use of cyberinfrastructure to tackle computational biology problems that would have been impossible to solve even a decade ago. As these developments progress, the availability of new diagnostic tests, drugs, and therapies will change how we prevent, find, and treat diseases such as cancer, influenza, and heart disease. These developments are not limited to physical health, either. Researchers' ability to use functional magnetic resonance imaging, single neuron recording, and other techniques (and to analyze, share, and archive the resulting data) has begun to change our fundamental understanding of the way the brain works. These developments could eventually help to address autism, depression, and other debilitating mental illnesses.

In industry, cyberinfrastructure is beginning to influence everything from energy extraction to nanoscale materials. The networked availability of detailed geological maps, satellite imagery, GPS coordinates, and other geographic information has begun to revolutionize every industry that depends on the movement of people and materials across the globe. The ability of large-scale distributed computing infrastructure to create realistic simulation models of nanoscale materials consisting of trillions of individual atoms has shortened the research and development processes in many companies that work with these tiny molecular structures. The promise of nanoscale structures in engineering transportation systems, biomaterials, information technology, and other areas promises to accelerate improvements and cost reductions in these areas.

Each of these areas has the potential for profound effects on our national and global economies, particularly with respect to global problems such as energy production and consumption, environmental degradation, overpopulation, and health in developing countries. Cyberinfrastructure systems, such as large-scale modeling applications, also have the potential to help improve economic forecasting, as well as give better predictions of the impact of proposed policy changes. Perhaps the most intriguing possibility arises from the interdisciplinary efforts that cyberinfrastructure can facilitate between economists, sociologists, psychologists, and other social scientists who can contribute to our understanding of large aggregates of people. Researchers in government and the military are already attempting to create simulation models of large-scale humanitarian problems such as the flow of refugees. With an improved ability to understand and predict the effects of natural and human-created events on the behavior and movements of large groupings of people, we may have future capabilities of averting problems in the national and global economies before they become disasters.

Perhaps the most important implication of cyberinfrastructure highlighted in the Atkins Report is the need for new and different kinds of education to prepare the swarms of professionals needed to imagine, develop, create, and maintain the gigantic amounts of cyberinfrastructure that the U.S. and other countries will need to maintain a high level of innovation and productivity. The report provides a general outline of the kind of skills and specialization that will be needed:

> The need for a new workforce—a new flavor of mixed science and technology professional—is emerging ... Needed in this interdisciplinary mix are professionals who are trained to understand and address the human factors dimensions of working across disciplines, cultures, and institutions using technology-mediated collaborative tools. (Atkins et al., 2003, p. 26)

This quote is the clarion call for this book. Although the U.S. has a robust range of educational programs that can educate individuals to have skills in the area of cyberinfrastructure, fewer and fewer U.S. students have chosen to take this path over recent years. Some students may feel that the curriculum is too difficult—that it requires too much math and too much scientific preparation—while others may imagine the work environment of an information professional as undesirable. As Chapter 5 suggested, some parents and students may believe that most jobs in the information sector have already gone offshore or will soon do so. In the next two chapters of this book, we seek to dispel some of these myths and to give a realistic and balanced overview of work in the information professions, as well as the educational preparation needed to enter those professions. The diversity of jobs, roles, and responsibilities may surprise you and perhaps inspire you to choose one of these paths for yourself or to influence another person to do so.

Endnotes

1. A timeline of Dan Atkins' career is available at www.si.umich.edu/images/faculty/atkins-timeline-2008.pdf.

2. Quoted from a newsletter archived at www.racinfo.indiana.edu/newsletter/archives/2007-03.shtml; copyright 2007 by The Trustees of Indiana University.

3. Note that images created by Wordle (www.wordle.net) are made available to the individuals who create them under a Creative Commons Attribution 3.0 U.S. License.

4. Visualization from Gapminder World, powered by Trendalyzer from www.gapminder.org.

References

Atkins, D. E., Droegemeier, K. K., Feldman, S. I., Garcia-Molina, H., Klein, M. L., Messerschmitt, D. G., et al. (2003). Revolutionizing science and engineering through cyberinfrastructure. *Report of the National Science Foundation blue-ribbon advisory panel on cyberinfrastructure*. Retrieved June 16, 2010, from www.nsf.gov/od/oci/reports/atkins.pdf

Iran's nonrepublic. (June 18, 2009). *New York Times*, p. A36.

CHAPTER 12

The Original Information Professionals

*Knowledge is of two kinds. We know a subject
ourselves, or we know where we can find information
upon it.*

—Samuel Johnson

In previous chapters, we have heard about the educational and work lives of a variety of current and future information professionals. In this chapter, we examine some of the ways library professionals, who are in effect the original information professionals, are involved in technologically advanced aspects of the information field and how hard-core technologists in the information field can and do connect with librarians. Library work is complex, and so are the skills needed to do it, and we take some time to describe the core competencies and personal attributes that modern librarians and other library professionals usually possess. Finally, we describe some important aspects of library education.

Unlike the image of librarians in TV and film, men and women who work in this field enjoy busy, challenging, and fulfilling work lives. Librarians interact with other professionals and with library users daily. They continually learn new technologies. Some manage highly complex projects. They have ample opportunity for leadership in their communities and in their professional organizations. For most, librarianship is a lifelong passion and not merely a job. As in medicine, social work, and public service, many roles in librarianship are focused on helping other people. Librarians form long-term social and professional relationships that are sustained through library organizations and profession-wide projects. Although most people know librarians who work behind a desk at a public library, many lesser-known subspecialties exist in the field, including work in hospitals, schools, museums, science research agencies, universities, and corporations.

For the purposes of this book, we are especially interested in how librarians interact with people, organizations, and technology in other parts of the information field. By introducing several librarians and sharing what they told us about their work, we hope to provide a realistic sense of what future information professionals can do in libraries (including digital libraries), the soft and hard skills and training students need to succeed, and the technologies that new professionals can expect to encounter early in their careers. Libraries and their information resources come in all shapes and sizes, and we have documented several unique situations in the pages that follow.

The evolution of librarianship and library work brings us into a world where information organization, information management, data quality curation and vetting, creation and maintenance of metadata, archiving, and so forth are not simply "helpful" (in the sense that a reference librarian is helpful) but are absolutely essential for a world that is both drowning in and highly dependent on information. We can see evidence of this in our discussions with librarians.

At the same time, librarians and information professionals are a unique breed. Jessamyn West describes it well when she says, "Librarianship is much more than a job. We're drawn to the information professions by a desire to help, a desire to serve, a desire to teach, and [a desire] to know. We stay in the profession despite decreasing funding, ever-changing job descriptions, and uncertain futures" (West, 2006).

We begin here with the stereotypes: the good, the bad, and the nerdy. We will show that the stereotypes of dusty libraries and cranky librarians just don't fit the present reality, and it is quite possible that they never did. "Although librarians have the reputation of being traditionalists wedded to books, they were actually very early adopters of computer technology" (Thompson, 2009). While some library environments are conservative and focused on preserving the past, more and more libraries and librarians are forward-looking, technology-friendly, and helping their organizations innovate into an exciting new world. As information experts, librarians have always had a strong incentive to try to be at the cutting edge, even when funding difficulties have made it challenging to keep up with the very rapid pace of IT change (Neal, 2009).

"Libraries are really exciting places and they are full of technology," says Jill Hurst-Wahl, an information school faculty member and a consultant in the Syracuse area. Her career has been characterized by bridging the intersection between information and technology. She became a librarian because she has always liked helping connect people with information, but she also felt excited about technology. She describes herself as tech friendly but purposely not on the bleeding edge, usually adopting new products only after other people have done some test-driving. As a consultant, she teaches her corporate clients how to choose and use the appropriate technologies to solve their information problems, most recently in the area of digitizing materials. "I like to see the light come on when people finally understand something. I like technology and learning how it can be applied."

In Chapter 2, we discussed how information tends toward disorganization. In fact, a central mission of most libraries and librarians is to keep information organized, accessible, and up to date. Many people think of the job types they see in plain view in public libraries, behind the reference or circulation desks, as typifying library work. However, there are many tasks and roles accomplished elsewhere that are also essential to helping the library fulfill its mission. A person does not even have to like books to enjoy library work (although many librarians do) because the work is so diverse. Hurst-Wahl points out that there is a great deal of activity that goes on behind the scenes with purchasing, contract negotiation, grant writing, preserving materials, evaluating software, and maintaining computer networks, to name a few.

Some of the tasks that librarians perform are not highly technological. Someone has to empty the drop box of all of the books, media, and sometimes even a kitten, such as the one named Dewey found by library director Vicki Myron (2009). Driving a bookmobile might also seem low-tech, although organizing the community activities done by the bookmobile staff requires extensive planning. Library jobs vary substantially in terms of technical skills needed and the amount of education required. Many fairly routine jobs, such as checking out books, require only a high school diploma. Maintaining systems and processes might call for a college degree in information technology or business administration. Leadership jobs, which are usually called professional, typically require a graduate degree. Most librarians who get graduate degrees begin working in libraries earlier in their careers and pursue a Master of Library Science (MLS) degree part-time while working. That process generally takes two or more years of part-time study. Entry-level salaries in libraries are generally lower than in business, but professional librarians, especially ambitious ones who plan their careers carefully, make salaries comparable to those of other public and private professionals. Recent data from the Bureau of Labor Statistics indicated that "the average annual salary for all librarians in the Federal Government in nonsupervisory, supervisory, and managerial positions was $80,873 in 2007."[1] Librarians who work in educational contexts tend to make more than public librarians, and those with managerial responsibilities frequently make more than those without.

A Day in the Life: Career Options in Library and Information Science (Shontz & Murray, 2007) showcases almost 100 examples of the day-to-day work lives and responsibilities of many kinds of librarians from public libraries, academic libraries, school libraries, special libraries, publishing companies, associations and agencies, and a variety of nontraditional organizations. For example, the book describes in detail how a GIS/data librarian, a university library director, a preservationist, a golf librarian, and an internet trainer spend their workdays. In one example, a multimedia librarian in a public library describes how she helps library users choose music and movies, how she deals with the ups and downs of working with the various people in her organization, and how a person could find a job like hers.

Assisting, educating, and informing—three hallmarks of librarianship—are all activities that require close interaction with people. "You had better get used to working with people" is how associate librarian Ron Foster describes the key to happiness in library work. He works at a state institute of technology and holds an MLS from the University of Albany. He describes his work as exciting and extremely people oriented. Most of the librarians he knows dread repetitive work, such as shelf reading, and thrive on solving puzzles and answering questions that most people would find challenging. Foster recalls a college class in which the professor assigned trivia questions (e.g., What's the last name of a famous cartoon character?), and the students would have to solve them, using as many different sources as there were questions. While most of us would stumble through many frustrating internet searches to answer this question, Foster made students aware of several valuable information resources unavailable on the internet and got great satisfaction from helping the students solve the puzzle efficiently.

Foster explained that sensitivity to people's body language and their subtle expressions of emotion is important to his job. The librarian's job is to assist, so it's important to notice how people react, how well they understand English, and whether they are following the point a person is trying to communicate. For example, the main job in the reference department is to help the user define his or her information need and then to recognize the precise moment when the user can take back control of solving the problem. Hurst-Wahl says, "You have to understand how to network with other people, how to listen to people around you and tell them how you can help them. You are often pointing out approaches to a problem and avoiding the use of complex technological language that might confuse the user.

Interestingly, this point is one that resonates with users of IT who have called on technical support for assistance and been baffled by the technology jargon used by IT personnel. Straightforward communication about complex problems is one area where librarians often excel, and it is a skill that needs to become more prominent throughout the information professions.

Diversity is an essential feature of libraries. Just as library patrons come from all walks of life, library professionals and staff pride themselves on the ability to work with people from a wide range of backgrounds. Many librarians receive special training to recognize variety in points of view and to understand how those differences affect information needs. "There is a lot of difference in opinion, ethnicity, culture, language and diversity in everything else. Librarians really appreciate that. The good news is they are accepting. The bad news is that people sometimes see this profession as an escape. They do social outreach and have a mission but have to act as a business too. It's just a gentler business," says Hurst-Wahl.

Researchers have taken note that some high school and college students seek out and relish opportunities for community engagement (Hart, Donnelly, Youniss, & Atkins, 2007; Kahne & Sporte, 2008). For those students whose passion is community building and increasing access to information resources and learning for members of the community, librarianship can be an attractive career option (Institute of Museum and Library Service, 2009). "Libraries build community in many ways," according to Laurie Brooks, an associate deputy director for library services. "Whether through preparing children for school, helping small businesses thrive, providing technology training for seniors, or imparting a new language, libraries are essential community resources in the Information Age."

Many librarians report that they share certain values with their co-workers and that their attraction to library work stemmed from these values. Library professionals often speak of a commitment to the freedom of information, an affinity for community, and a belief in equality of access for all people. Librarians value IT for its role in furthering the mission to provide access to information. A fierce curiosity and a drive to solve problems also energize many librarians. "You have to enjoy the hunt," Hurst-Wahl explains. "A good hunter can pick up on clues, knows something about the lay of the land, understands what has worked in the past and will in the future: important skills for research." People who enjoy puzzles and details can thrive in an environment, especially but not limited to reference work, where hunting for tidbits of information is a routine and important activity.

The personal attributes that many librarians possess and that enhance their roles as information facilitators (curiosity, mental agility, and helpfulness) are remarkably different from the common stereotype of the "librarian with a bun." Librarians are often portrayed in the media in their role as gatekeepers between people and information. Ruth Kneale's book *You Don't Look Like a Librarian* (2009) shatters these negative stereotypes, including those of librarians as shy and socially incompetent. Kneale explains how these stereotypes have negatively affected the librarian image—in the ways patrons treat them, in the undervaluing of their work, and in lost opportunities to help people because of the patrons' own biases against library professionals who do not fit the image (p. 3). Library patrons, both students and community members in general, miss out on great opportunities by undervaluing the skills of the library workers who could help them.

Librarians all over have banded together to shatter the limited views of the general public. Some illustrative examples include the Bellydancing Librarians, the Butt Kicking Librarians (martial artists), the Facebook Librarians, the Laughing Librarian (with librarian jokes), the Lipstick Librarian, the Modified Librarian (referring to tattoos), and the Radical Reference librarians (Kneale, 2009, pp. 106–115). The Tattooed Ladies of the Texas Library Association (www.txla.org/temp/tattoo.html) publish a calendar of women's "concealed art" to raise funds for disaster relief, an unambiguous testament to their mission to "thrive on and promote diversity and freedom of expression." Another rather flashy example of efforts to refute stereotypes is the Librarian Book Cart Drill Championships held annually at American Library Association meetings. Teams of librarians in Viking costumes and other garb compete for a golden library cart. The sheer silliness of this endeavor is not lost on the event's organizers, according to Mo Willems in an NPR interview. "There's a stereotype that librarians are boring," she says. "And I think they want to change that stereotype to 'librarians are crazy'" (quoted in Spitzer, 2009).

For all this craziness and stereotype-busting fun, there is one critical characteristic that librarians share with other information professionals: the generalist's ability to learn new technologies at the drop of a hat. Thompson (2009) describes this by saying that one of the main competencies of librarianship is to "give up the concept of mastery" (p. 22). Technologies change so quickly that the specific software and tools learned in coursework may not exist once a new graduate starts a job. Hurst-Wahl explains that continuing to take IT courses after graduation is essential. In her words, "IT classes can be hard, but you need to take some. It is the ground floor for everything that you need to learn. I learned languages that are no longer used, and that is OK. You need that base. You may hate it, but it's the price of admission. You have to like technology. It's not just using it, but understanding how it works and how it used to work is sometimes important too." Versatility is a requirement of librarianship. In Hurst-Wahl's words, "The number of directions that people can go is unlimited. It's not just programming networks, it's research, handling contracts, negotiating. It is a good degree to have. You can make a career wherever you want."

It is easy to underestimate the amount and complexity of the information technology that goes into the running of even an average-sized library, but it makes sense when a person considers that a library is a premier example of an information organization. In *Library Technology Companion: A Basic Guide for Library Staff*, John J. Burke (2006) summarizes the main technologies a library worker is likely to encounter, including computers (such as laptops, tablets, and handheld devices); software (such as library systems, open source, and office productivity applications); storage devices, library databases and electronic resources; search tools; blogging and other social software; local area networking for tying together the library's equipment; and wide area networking for participating in regional and national library services. The design, development, and maintenance of this infrastructure require people who work in libraries to possess various combinations of IT, telecommunications, and library skills. Library workers put these technologies to work, ensuring accessibility, providing virtual reference support, and handling classroom technologies. Problems of space, infrastructure, and employee/user well being enter into the picture as well.

"Technology pervades my job," says Foster. "When there is no power in the building, we can't even find a book. When the databases are down or students want help, there is very little that can be done." According to Foster, one of the coolest things about his job is that he can sit in his office and control another computer, a dedicated server that handles interlibrary loan, and can find out the location of a book and request it from anywhere in the country within minutes. Articles that used to take weeks to arrive now show up as an image file within hours. Of course, Foster and his colleagues must understand more than just the technology itself. Their essential role is to know how libraries organize their information, using technology as an aid in that process. A recent innovation in this field is that computers are making advances in the library's ability to balance the work/service loads of different libraries, resulting in better service for everyone. Of course, the goal is not technology itself but rather the provision of information needed by the library user.

"There is no way the library can function without the behind-the-scenes work of IT people like our recently hired programmer analyst," explains Foster. With a bachelor's degree in computer science, he assists staff by responding directly to their requests for help, sets up the systems (computers, servers) that make the library run, and helps with planning for the future, such as deciding what technology needs are necessary and affordable for the reference section.

In fact, planning for future IT innovations is an essential role in library organizations. Burke (2006) forecasts a "complex library" for the future and outlines some key trends. For example, future libraries will struggle with achieving a balance between electronic and print resources, finding ways for patrons to access new (and expensive) information resources, and developing ways to interact with patrons online and in person (Burke, 2006, p. 204). The increased availability of ebooks, the introduction of nontraditional copyright controls, the provision of blogging and related user-driven content as viable information services, the emergence of folksonomies (classification systems using regular language), and greater reliance on digital reference will all have a profound influence on the library of the future. Radio frequency identification (RFID) technology for automated sorting, inventory, and self-checkout has already made its entrance into libraries, along with a whole set of related concerns about privacy and the changing roles of librarians. For a full discussion of emerging technologies and the future of the academic library, we recommend Li's (2009) work, *Emerging Technologies for Academic Libraries in the Digital Age*, which gives real-world examples of highly innovative and potentially revolutionary technologies.

Many of us recognize that social networking and crowdsourcing tools, what some people refer to as Web 2.0, will continue to have an impact on libraries. New jobs in this environment will likely emerge to help handle social networking, wikis, mashups, podcasts, gaming, and library activities (Courtney, 2007). Some of these activities will take place in virtual as well as real, physical library spaces. The current generation of students who will seek jobs in the coming few years will have skills in these areas and the expectation that their employers will take advantage of those skills. In Foster's words, "They use social technology like a fish swims in water." Libraries are already incorporating many of these social networking principles and tools into the mix. Burke (2006) expects that the need for library staff trained in IT and dedicated to providing such new complex IT tasks will surely increase. As libraries' dependence on IT grows, so will the need for people to help with these critical technologies.

A variety of educational paths can lead to a technology-intensive job in a library environment. Support of computer systems, installation of new software and hardware, and maintenance of equipment might be done by someone with a two-year degree. Supervision in this area often requires a four-year degree. Middle or upper management of a library's technology functions could require an undergraduate degree in IT combined with an MLS degree. For highly specialized areas, such as medical librarianship, an individual might even have two master's degrees, perhaps one in biology and one in library science. This pattern holds in other research settings as well. Many librarians have work backgrounds in other areas, such as supply-chain management or technology development, and they combine the skills they learned in those areas with library training to redefine their career paths.

The future will probably have more spots for librarians such as Susan Skrien, who is the manager of library and reference for a large online university. Her MLS degree has helped her navigate her new role: providing library services to more than 20,000 adult learners in an online-only digital library environment. She collaborates with curriculum specialists and course developers to provide online information literacy instruction. She supervises other librarians and works with online design teams to create online tutorials and modules about library use. Because her organization has a goal to double enrollment to 50,000 learners by 2013, strategic planning to manage that growth from a library perspective is crucial. To keep her skills sharp and to stay in touch with the virtual library's expansive user community, Skrien answers email and phone reference calls for a four-hour shift every week. She uses technology to create and manage the reference schedule. She issues a quarterly online newsletter for faculty, in which she reports on technological changes affecting her organization. Social networking and other Web 2.0 tools, such as shared bookmarking and shared bibliographic management tools, have become more important in this environment as well. Skrien says, "Overall, my job has a lot to do with learning, teaching, coaching others, administration, and making decisions. It's a fantastic job, and I'm very satisfied by the work that I do."

Skrien's unique job highlights the fact that about two-thirds of librarians work in environments other than the traditional public library. The Special Libraries Association (SLA) website[2] indicates that there are more than 34,000 special libraries around the world. This huge set of organizations includes "research libraries, information centers, archives, and data centers maintained by government agencies, business, industry, newspapers, educational institutions, nonprofit organizations, and societies in the fields of science and engineering, medicine, law, art, religion, the social sciences, and humanities." Because of the enormous variety of missions and focus areas, special libraries can be exciting places to work. In addition to special libraries dedicated to topics such as medicine, law, or sciences, here is a small sampling of unusual and intriguing special libraries along with the focus topics of their collections:

- The National Baseball Hall of Fame Library in Cooperstown, New York, focuses on baseball.

- The New York Yacht Club Library focuses on sailing and boats.

- The Academy of Motion Picture Arts and Sciences Library in Beverly Hills focuses on cinema.

- The Maine Maritime Museum Library in Bath, focuses on maritime history.

- The American Museum of Natural History Library in New York focuses on natural history and ecology.

- The *New York Times* Library and Morgue is a reference library for newspapers.

- The National Public Radio Library in Washington, DC, is a reference library for radio.

- The William E. Colby Memorial Library of the Sierra Club focuses on nature and mountaineering.

Special libraries also exist nested within much larger library organizations, and these often house unusual, rare, and sometimes completely strange collections of documents and other materials. For example, Tulane University has a collection of catalog covers for seeds, a jazz history collection, and a carnival collection with historical information about float designs throughout history. The Princeton University Library has a circus poster collection. The New York Public Library owns a large collection of tobacco-related ephemera. Historical documents about frauds, hoaxes, and counterfeiting from a variety of different time periods can be found in the Frank W. Tober Collection on Literary Forgery at the University of Delaware. Duke University's collection has papyri from ancient Egypt, a set of literary accounts of utopian communities, and collections of comic books, newspaper cartoons, and feminist zines. The Sealaska Heritage Institute has a library that holds publications and images of the history, culture, and languages of the people of Southeast Alaska. A collection of 425 nursing romance novels exists at the University of Wisconsin-Milwaukee. Some of the collections are for listening, such as the Judaica Sound Archive at Florida Atlantic University. These and other surprising collections are described in Kristin Ohlson's (2009) article on the Smithsonian website.

Several years ago, a group of journalists had the opportunity to visit the top-secret Animation Research Library ("Touring the Disney Animated Research Library," 2006). The original story sketches for *Lady and the Tramp* and recorded interviews with actors such as Don Dunagan, otherwise known as "the voice of Bambi," are housed in this library. Librarians there are involved in making materials accessible for clients, preparing and delivering Disney-related exhibitions, contributing to the digital restoration of classic films, and collecting and preserving rare and extremely valuable materials. One project has restored and scanned more than 1,000 paper story backgrounds that were rolled up in empty ice cream containers for decades. In addition to working on the main collection, information professionals work in the DVD production area, finding and reproducing artwork and historical materials for bonus features.

The Internet Archive (IA; www.archive.org), located in San Francisco, is a futuristic library with the mission of preserving and providing access to collections of digital data. This "internet library" contains texts, audio, movies, software, and archived webpages. Music lovers especially might enjoy the behind-the-scenes work necessary in running IA operations, which houses more than 56,000 live concerts. The Grateful Dead collection alone contains nearly 7,000 items. At the time of this writing, the IA was seeking new personnel including experts in digital conversion, data crawl engineers, and various other information personnel to capture data, analyze current practices, and experiment with "harvesting techniques" for future evolution of the IA. According to Hurst-Wahl, other digital libraries, such as the World Digital Library (Library of Congress and UNESCO), open up new possibilities for combining text, digital audio, digital photography, digital video, and maps. Librarians will play a role in integrating these materials from separate silos to enhance their availability and accessibility (e.g., making materials available on mobile devices). Eventually, these capabilities will evolve to provide position-sensitive information resources that users can obtain and use on mobile phones.

The maintenance and care of these information resources fulfills a deep societal need to distribute, maintain, and preserve the many written and recorded elements of our heritage. UNESCO and the International Federation of Library Associations and Institutions have launched two declarations of principles to guide the creation and operations of public libraries and school libraries worldwide. The Public Library Manifesto, adopted in 1994, proclaims UNESCO's belief in the public library as a living force for education, culture, and information and "an essential agent for the fostering of peace and spiritual welfare through the minds of men and women."[3] Along those same lines, the School Library Manifesto, which was adopted in 1999, defines and advances the role of school libraries and resource centers in enabling students to acquire the tools and content that allows them to develop their full capacities, to continue to learn throughout their lives, and to make informed decisions.

As this rich array of examples shows, librarianship is in the midst of a rapid evolution from a profession concerned mainly with books inside brick buildings into a multifaceted set of roles that requires innovative thinking, broad knowledge of IT, and a dedicated commitment to helping people access information. The librarian's job within and outside of the traditional library is changing rapidly, especially with developments in new information technologies. Educational preparation for these jobs is, necessarily, changing as well.

For decades, library jobs existed on just two levels: support and professional. The latter, involving information organization and delivery, required a master's degree. Today, the range of jobs is much broader. While student librarians are learning more about new technologies, libraries also need workers of many kinds whose skills reside primarily in technology. Many colleges and universities have programs at the undergraduate level for information management and related technologies. A few universities have schools that offer both undergraduate programs in this area and the traditional MLS, a point we will discuss in greater detail in Chapter 13. A few even have PhD programs in the theoretical aspects of information science. Professional education programs respond to employment needs, and it is clear that new "information" jobs in libraries, or library-like institutions, require a significant amount of technological expertise. The essential importance of this expertise is reflected in the definition of an information professional offered by the SLA. According to the SLA, an information professional is a person who "strategically uses information in his/her job to advance the mission of the organization. This is accomplished through the development, deployment, and management of information resources and services. The [information professional] harnesses technology as a critical tool to accomplish goals. [Information professionals] include, but are not limited to, librarians, knowledge managers, chief information officers, web developers, information brokers, and consultants."[4] The key roles for information professionals include the following:

- Developing and maintaining a portfolio of cost-effective, client-valued information services that are aligned with the strategic directions of the organization and client groups

- Building a dynamic collection of information resources based on a deep understanding of clients' information needs

- Gathering evidence to support decisions about the development of new services and products

- Maintaining current awareness of emerging technologies

- Assessing and communicating the value of the information organization, including information services and products and policies to senior management, key stakeholders, and client groups

- Contributing effectively to senior management strategies and decisions regarding information applications, tools and technologies, and policies for the organization[5]

Note that this list requires a balanced mixture of so-called hard skills (e.g., technology-related) and soft skills (e.g., interpersonal communication). The hard skills, which can change rapidly, need to be learned as a foundation for anything that will come in the future: basic computer hardware, operating systems, office productivity software, basic system troubleshooting, digitizing, electronic database searching, blogs, wikis, evaluating websites, creating tutorials, digital cameras, and peripherals (Neal, 2009, p. 47). Soft skills include oral and written communication, presentation, negotiation, small group interaction, personnel supervision, and project management. If you have been reading the rest of this book, you might find it quite striking that these lists of hard and soft skills are nearly identical to what employers in corporations, governments, and other settings are expecting from their information workers in jobs that have *never* been considered librarian jobs. We believe this similarity is indicative of a convergence of core skills in the information professions. This skills convergence reflects the fact that people everywhere are trying to solve important problems with information and technology. Librarians currently have and have always possessed a key set of skills in this area, particularly in knowing how to organize information, answer questions, and make information resources available to others. Add these critical skills to a broad knowledge of the underlying technological infrastructure of most modern organizations, and you have the essential information professional who is needed across a huge variety of current and emerging jobs in every sector of society. In the remaining chapters of this book, we will discuss the educational options for becoming a "converged" information professional and what each student can do to prepare for challenging, interesting, and well-paying information jobs.

Endnotes

1. "Librarians: Earnings," Bureau of Labor Statistics, stats.bls.gov/oco/ocos068.htm#earnings (accessed August 5, 2009).

2. "General Industry FAQs," Special Libraries Association, www.sla.org/content/membership/Genfaq.cfm (accessed August 5, 2009).

3. "IFLA/UNESCO Public Library Manifesto 1994," archive.ifla.org/VII/s8/unesco/eng.htm (accessed March 15, 2010).

4. "Association Profile," Special Libraries Association, www.sla.org/content/SLA/AssnProfile/index.cfm (accessed July 26, 2009).

5. Ibid.

References

Burke, J. J. (2006). *Library technology companion: A basic guide for library staff.* New York: Neal-Shulman.

Cohen, M. (2007). Mulitimedia librarian. In P. Shontz & R. Murray (Eds.), *A day in the life: Career options in library and information science.* Westport, CT: Libraries Unlimited.

Courtney, N. (2007). *Library 2.0 and beyond: Innovative technologies and tomorrow's user.* Westport, CT: Libraries Unlimited.

Hart, D., Donnelly, T. M., Youniss, J., & Atkins, R. (2007). High school community service as a predictor of adult voting and volunteering. *American Educational Research Journal, 44*(1), 197.

Institute of Museum and Library Service. (2009). IMLS report: Libraries are a vital community resource in the Information Age [press release]. Retrieved August 5, 2009, from www.imls.gov/news/2009/070109.shtm

Kahne, J. E., & Sporte, S. E. (2008). Developing citizens: The impact of civic learning opportunities on students' commitment to civic participation. *American Educational Research Journal, 45*(3), 738.

Kneale, R. (2009). *You don't look like a librarian: Shattering stereotypes and creating positive new images in the internet age.* Medford, NJ: Information Today.

Li, L. (2009). *Emerging technologies for academic libraries in the digital age.* Oxford, UK: Chandos.

Myron, V., & Witter, B. (2008). *Dewey: The small town library cat who touched the world.* New York: Grand Central.

Neal, D. (2009). The library school's role in preparing new librarians for working with technology. In S. M. Thompson (Ed.), *Core technology competencies for librarians and library staff.* New York: Neal-Shuman.

Ohlson, K. (March 1, 2009). Libraries' surprising special collections. Smithsonian.com. Retrieved March 15, 2010, from www.smithsonian mag.com/arts-culture/Libraries-Surprising-Special-Collections.html

Ostler, L. J., Dahlin, T. C., & Willardson, J. D. (1995). *The closing of American library schools: Problems and opportunities.* Westport, CT: Greenwood Press.

Shontz, P., & Murray, R. (Eds). (2007). *A day in the life: Career options in library and information science.* Westport, CT: Libraries Unlimited.

Spitzer, G. (July 13, 2009). Librarians go wild for gold book cart. NPR. Retrieved July 26, 2009, from www.npr.org/templates/story/story.php?storyId=106561675&sc=nl&cc=es-20090728

Thompson, S. M. (2009). *Core technology competencies for librarians and library staff.* New York: Neal-Shuman.

Touring the Disney Animated Research Library: A report from an undisclosed location. (February 26, 2006). UltimateDisney.com. Retrieved June 15, 2009, from www.ultimatedisney.com/arltour.html

West, J. (2006). Introduction: What do librarians do all day? In P. Shontz & R. Murray (Eds.), *A day in the life: Career options in library and information science.* Westport, CT: Libraries Unlimited.

CHAPTER 13

To iSchool or Not to iSchool

What's in a name?

—William Shakespeare

When we think of gangs, we usually imagine batches of tough young thugs causing trouble out on the streets. But one gang, started in 1988, consisted of a reasonably well-mannered group of mid-level academic administrators—deans, to be precise—who set out to refine the education of professionals in the field of information. The original Gang of Three, founded by Dr. Toni Carbo, who was at that time dean of the School of Information Sciences at the University of Pittsburgh, expanded over a period of 15 years to a Gang of Ten that included some of the most influential academic leaders in the information field. Carbo and her colleagues anticipated many of the changes that the information professions would undergo as computers and networks became more ubiquitous and cheaper and as information moved from print materials stored in the library to digital media hosted in computer servers. For example, in an early publication titled, "The Changing Role of the Information Professional" (1984), Carbo offered the following ideas:

> I believe that we are entering [an era] of individual-oriented
> or customized information services. We are designing and
> repackaging products and services for individuals, either at
> home or in business and industry. This era introduces

exciting new challenges for information professionals, to
identify individual user's needs, develop new products,
and market and sell them. (pp. 256–267)

On the surface, the prediction in 1984 of a new genre of information services seems quite unadventurous until we reflect on the fact
that the World Wide Web was not due for another 10 years and the
IBM personal computer had been available only for three. When
Carbo wrote that article, only a handful of people anywhere in the
world were imagining that customized, individualized web services
such as Yahoo! Answers or Wikipedia were even possible, let alone
commonplace and essentially free, as they are now. In the same article, Carbo also forecasted some necessary changes in the education
of information professionals:

If we set out today to design a curriculum to educate
information professionals for the [future] what would we
put in it? Courses on organization theory, financial planning, strategic planning, and effective communications
should be included. Much more interaction with business
schools and departments of communication is also
important. (p. 259)

In the first section of this book, we explored the forces that cause
some information jobs to be outsourced or offshored while other jobs
remain resistant to these forces. Among those that are not exportable
are jobs that require skills drawn from more than one discipline.
Taken with Carbo's quote, this material suggests that a new kind of
education was needed, combining a variety of skills to prepare workers for businesses, government, education, healthcare, and other sectors. Of course, each information professional will need to
understand key essentials of information itself: Information representation, metadata, classification, and retrieval are a few of the basic
areas. However, to take full advantage of the power provided by
cyberinfrastructure and to be able to meld existing and emerging

technologies in exciting new ways, the future information professional will also have to be a technology generalist, capable of deftly navigating the various layers of networks, databases, processing, and user interfaces that comprise the information technology of today and tomorrow. Simultaneously, the future information professional will need expertise in one or more areas of the human sciences, including perception, individual motivation and behavior, communication, instructional design, human-computer interaction, small group behavior, organizational change, interorganizational relations, institutional theory, and economics. This is a tall order. No undergraduate student can expect to master all of these areas in four years of study.

What many students do not realize prior to researching their options for college (and sometimes even after they get to college) is that a different and more focused educational program is available in some universities where the liberal arts model of education is dominant. These programs are offered in professional schools. *Schools of information* represent an emerging example of a new professional school.

The best known professional school offering undergraduate majors is the business school. As we discussed earlier in the book, more than 300,000 individuals graduate with bachelor's degrees in business from U.S. colleges and universities each year; business schools are the most prevalent source of professional education in the country, based purely on popularity. Business schools represent just the tip of the iceberg in professional education, though. Other historically favored choices for professional majors include journalism, health and human services, nursing, and education, while other areas, such as protective services, recreation/leisure studies, and engineering technology have gradually become better known over the past few decades. These professional schools provide a focused educational experience that prepares a student for entry-level (associate's or bachelor's), mid-level (master's), or high-level (doctoral) positions in the given occupational area. For undergraduates, most professional schools require a breadth of coursework that includes elements of the traditional general education curriculum. For example, almost all undergraduate students in business schools must complete writing courses to fulfill their degree requirements. However, even after taking these courses into account, professional education at most schools frequently provides a more centered and specialized level of career preparation than traditional majors such as history or sociology. Within the university as a whole, professional schools often have some latitude to customize their offerings for undergraduate students, and this can include relaxing some of the common general education requirements of the liberal arts program (e.g., literature or language) in favor of additional coursework in the occupational area. Professional schools often lead the way in hands-on experience as well, with required internships or community service providing the most common examples of how students can obtain relevant pre-professional experience.

There is a new kid on the block in professional education. The increasing importance of information (as we have discussed in earlier parts of this book) has led to the establishment of a small number of specialized programs that focus on the information professions. A group of these schools has adopted the letter "i" as its abbreviation, leading to the moniker *iSchool*, echoing the common usage of *bSchool* in reference to business school and *jSchool* in reference to journalism school. The following overview was taken from the website of the iSchools, an organization representing some of these schools:

> The iSchools are interested in the relationship [among] information, people, and technology. This is characterized by a commitment to learning and understanding the role of information in human endeavors. The iSchools take it as a given that expertise in all forms of information is required for progress in science, business, education, and culture. This expertise must include understanding of the uses and users of information, as well as information technologies and their applications.[1]

This overview captures the significance of the many applications of information across the professions, as we discussed in Chapter 3, as well as the approach that the iSchools take regarding the relative importance of users and technology. In fact, elsewhere on the iSchools website, as well as on many of the sites of the individual schools, a trio of "information, technology, and people" is often indicated as the primary concern of the iSchools. These new iSchools pepper the U.S., from West Coast schools such as the School of Information at the University of California, Berkeley and the Donald Bren School of Information and Computer Sciences at the University of California, Irvine, all the way to East Coast schools such as the College of Information Studies at the University of Maryland and the College of Information Sciences and Technology at The Pennsylvania State University. Recently, educational institutions with similar goals in other countries have begun to join this emerging group, including the School of Information Management at Wuhan University in China and the Information Studies program at the University of Sheffield in England. Note that many other institutions exist with goals and principles similar to those described here but without calling themselves iSchools. We have provided a partial list of such institutions in Appendix C. To date, membership in the group of iSchools has only included schools that have substantial research activities in addition to an educational focus on the information professions. Hopefully in the near future, the organization will include a wider range of schools, including programs where teaching is the primary mission. Here is the list of all iSchools as of July 2010:

University of California, Berkeley: School of Information
University of California, Irvine: The Donald Bren School of Information and Computer Sciences
University of California, Los Angeles: Graduate School of Education and Information Studies
Carnegie Mellon University: School of Information Systems and Management, Heinz College
Drexel University: College of Information Science and Technology

Florida State University: College of Communication and Information

Georgia Institute of Technology: College of Computing

Humboldt-Universität zu Berlin: Berlin School of Library and Information Science

University of Illinois: Graduate School of Library and Information Science

Indiana University: School of Informatics and Computing

Indiana University: School of Library and Information Science

University of Maryland: College of Information Studies

University of Maryland, Baltimore County: Department of Information Systems

University of Michigan: School of Information

University of North Carolina: School of Information and Library Science

University of North Texas: College of Information

The Pennsylvania State University: College of Information Sciences and Technology

University of Pittsburgh: School of Information Sciences

Royal School of Library and Information Science, Denmark

Rutgers, The State University of New Jersey: School of Communication and Information

University of Sheffield, England: Information Studies

Singapore Management University: School of Information Systems

Syracuse University: School of Information Studies

University of Texas, Austin: School of Information

University of Toronto: Faculty of Information

University of Washington: Information School

Wuhan University, China: School of Information Management

Some of the current crop of iSchools started out as graduate library schools. Library schools traditionally did not offer undergraduate degrees, and their focus was naturally on training people specifically for employment in libraries. As these schools expanded the scope of their educational activities to include information technology, telecommunications, networking, and other areas, they began to change their names to reflect this wider focus. In 1974, Syracuse University became the first to completely drop the word *library* from its name as it changed from the School of Library Science to the School of Information Studies. The University of Michigan went a step further in 1996, simplifying the name of its library school to the School of Information. Recently, the program at Rutgers University shortened its name from School of Communication Information and Library Studies to simply School of Communication and Information. Despite the name changes, many of these schools have kept their graduate library programs as an essential core of their offerings and identities.

Others among the iSchools do not have roots in library education. For example, Indiana University's School of Informatics and Computing, founded in 1999, had no formal connection to the university's library science program when it was created, although the informatics faculty and library faculty do intersect now. The University of Washington's Information School (iSchool) and The Pennsylvania State University's College of Information Sciences and Technology were developed "from scratch" with no foundation in a previously existing academic unit.

John King, dean of the School of Information at the University of Michigan, summed up the state of the emerging movement in 2006:

> iSchools have been born in a state of flux, and in most cases have added to that flux through ongoing innovation. There is no rest in this process. The iSchool movement is emergent; its equilibrium can only be found in an essential tension among competing visions in a world of rapid technical and social change. iSchool identity is elusive and will remain so for the foreseeable future. (p. 13)

King's judgment is that these schools do not have a universally accepted identity at present in contrast to law schools and medical schools. This idea probably extends beyond the iSchools to all of the

various programs that educate students for the information professions. The professional world of information and technology is in a
state of constant advancement. If the information field and the curriculum used to educate new professionals for the field were fixed, as
could be the case if these schools had a cohesive identity, they might
quickly become obsolete. The current group of 20 to 30 iSchools is
highly diverse, with a huge range of educational backgrounds represented by each school's current group of faculty. Looking beyond the
iSchools, there is even greater diversity in the educational approaches
taken by other schools of information and technology. Both the rate of
change and the range of options may be dizzying, but there is also
something invigorating about the opportunity to "get in on the ground
floor" of something that may become notable. Ten or 20 years hence,
when schools of information are perhaps as common as business
schools or law schools, some early alumni will have the bragging
rights to say that they were there at the start of the movement.

For students who are considering working in the information
fields, it is important to think through the many options carefully. In
Chapter 11, we reported on some of the options for future librarians
at all levels of education. For other information professionals, the
same rule applies. There are some information jobs a person can perform with two- or four-year degrees (e.g., web design, project management, some types of network management), while other types of
jobs may require a master's degree (e.g., information security management, network design, policy, standards decisions). Teaching and
research-oriented jobs, as well as consulting and some information
leadership jobs, usually require a PhD. Students interested in the
information professions have many programs from which to choose
at each of these levels.

We have briefly described the evolution of the iSchools and how
they emphasize the social context of information together with the
technology. This approach requires thinking in an interdisciplinary
way and is most suitable for those students whose interests lie at the
intersection of information, technology, people, and organizations.
For students who wish to focus more on the social and humanistic

aspects of the information professions and less on the technology, programs focusing on human-computer interaction, information design, and technical communications might be most suitable. Students who have greater interest in the development and deployment of technology might choose telecommunications, networking, or information security programs.

In addition to considering whether a degree program focuses mainly on information, technology, people, organizations, or a mix of all of those topics, one must also take into account the amount of structure the program provides. The iSchools are in some ways very new, and they have as yet not wholly agreed among themselves on what constitutes a universal curriculum for the education of new information professionals. Some schools, such as the University of Michigan's iSchool, encourage students to tailor their education to fit their interests and offer suggested pathways into professions such as usability specialist, search engineer, system analyst, digital curator, or government archivist. Other schools, such as the Donald Bren School of Information and Computer Sciences at the University of California, Irvine, have degree programs that offer highly structured paths for students through the curriculum. The Bren School's undergraduate degree in business information management has all four years of the degree well planned out; typically students only need to choose one elective or breadth requirement each quarter.

Another important consideration is the background of the faculty. In established disciplines such as history or sociology, many faculty members agree on what should be taught at an introductory level, and virtually every faculty member has mastered the essential knowledge in those introductory areas. In contrast, because the information field is so broad and because it is changing so rapidly, faculty members must work that much harder to develop generalized knowledge of the field. For example, many specialists in human-computer interaction have minimal knowledge of networking, and vice versa, yet most students probably need an introduction to both. Larger schools may have the luxury of having experts in a variety of areas, while smaller schools must choose their focus area more carefully.

Students who are deciding on a program should examine the educational background and teaching experience of the faculty in each school to make sure that student interests and faculty expertise match.

Courses, homework, projects, and papers provide only one part of each student's educational experience, however. So when choosing a program, it makes sense to look beyond the quality and appropriateness of academic offerings. Participation in student organizations helps students develop their future professional network, learn about other students' experiences, and work on projects outside of formal coursework. The School of Information Studies at Syracuse University, for example, has undergraduate student organizations such as the Black and Latino Information Science and Technology Support group, the oldest such group in the U.S., which provides mentoring, networking, and community action activities for its members.

In the same vein, the presence of the undergraduate programs alongside graduate programs creates an interesting educational dynamic. At some schools, undergraduates, graduate students, and faculty share the same building spaces and are involved in collaborative projects together. For example, the School of Information at the University of California, Berkeley, has two centers that bring together students and other members of that intellectual community, namely, the center for Information Service and Design and the center for Information and Communication Technologies and Development, focusing on developing regions. These schools encourage students at all levels to join professional organizations, attend conferences, and participate in the intellectual and social life of their chosen subfields before graduation. They pride themselves on forging relationships among students, faculty, and practitioners and encouraging interdisciplinary partnerships. For example, Drexel University's College of Information Science and Technology has three undergraduate degree programs, three master's degree programs, and a PhD program. Drexel's faculty teaches across all three of these levels and involves undergraduates, master's, and doctoral students in their projects. Paid and volunteer internships, alternative spring breaks (service-oriented projects), and other ways to get involved in community life are also options at some schools.

Information schools conduct research in many areas, and evidence of this can be found in the number and quality of research grants received by their faculty and the subsequent publication records. For example, the Center for Pervasive Communications and Computing at the University of California, Irvine, which is dedicated to advances in wearable computers, receives many grants from industry. The Center for Emergency Response Technologies, dedicated to saving lives and property, is also located at Irvine. Syracuse University's Center for Natural Language Processing, where language and technology experts build software that helps people and organizations make the best use of documents and other text, receives grants from foundations and the federal government. Likewise, Syracuse's Center for Digital Literacy conducts funded research on programs that examine media literacy among children and adults. Many other research centers exist as well, such as the Center for Data and Search Informatics at Indiana University's School of Informatics and Computing and The Pennsylvania State University's Center for Human-Computer Interaction, and many of these centers provide opportunities for students to become involved in research.

One specific annual conference showcases the newest research and teaching innovations by faculty and students in the information fields: the iConference. The 2009 iConference website[2] lists topics including cultural information systems, globalization, and information management, organization, and policy. The conference is held at an iSchool in a different part of the country every year, with the 2009 event at the University of North Carolina and 2010 at the University of Illinois at Champaign-Urbana. The keynote address for each iConference, such as the 2009 speech by University of North Carolina's Chancellor Holden Thorp, can be found on YouTube.[3] Thorp's speech, titled "The 21st Century Knowledge Worker," provides interesting insights into how one academic leader views the information professions.

Program websites provide some of the best basic information on each program, and we have provided a list of websites for many of the schools in the information field in Appendix C. In addition, students who are primarily interested in the interdisciplinary iSchools can begin by consulting the iSchools website (www.ischools.org). When examining the degree offerings, courses, and faculty for any information program, students can use the following short checklist of questions:

- How much does this program emphasize studying technology, especially relative to how much it focuses on people?

- What kinds of technology skills will I learn? The web? Databases? Networks? Operating systems? What else?

- What kinds of nontechnology skills will I learn? General management? Project management? User studies? Information design? Information economics? What else?

- What kinds of pre-professional experiences, such as internships, will be available to me during my course of study? Are these required or optional, and how much support does the school give in finding these opportunities?

- Where do most of the program graduates go? Into financial services companies? Underwriting and insurance companies? Management consulting companies? Internet startups? Where else?

One final issue we should address concerns the rankings of schools. There are many controversies surrounding college ranking, including concerns with how the rankings are constructed and difficulties with some measures such as "institutional reputation" (University of Illinois Library, 2009). Even schools with high rankings sometimes admit that their rankings do not mean much. Further, some top schools, such as the Harvard Business School, have declined to participate in the ranking process, even knowing that they would most likely be at or near the top of the list. We strongly agree with these concerns and advise prospective students of information schools to ignore the rankings of different programs. Universities, colleges, degree programs, and faculty are simply too complex to be reduced to a single position on a ranking list. It is a false comfort for a student to say, "I got into a top-ranked school," because so much of the educational experience depends upon the path the student takes through a school rather than the school itself. When students conduct research on which schools to apply to, we suggest that they cast a wide net for information about what would best suit them as individual learners. The geographic location of a school, the size and interests of its faculty, the amount of financial aid the school can offer, and the specifics of the curriculum all matter much more than a school's rankings.

In the remaining chapters of this book, we consider the steps you should take to prepare, assuming that you are a student who is interested in entering a degree program in the information professions.

Endnotes

1. iSchools home page, www.ischools.org (accessed July 29, 2009).
2. iConferences home page, www.ischools.org/iconferences/2009index (accessed July 29, 2009).
3. Speech at 2009 iConference by University of North Carolina's Chancellor Holden Thorp, YouTube, www.youtube.com/watch?v=7C-UJtjyKkM (accessed July 29, 2009).

References

Carbo (Bearman), T. C. (1984). The changing role of the information professional. *Library Trends, 32*(3), 255–260.

King, J. L. (2006). Identity in the I-school movement. *Bulletin of the American Society for Information Science and Technology, 32*(4), 13–15.

University of Illinois Library. (2009). College and university rankings: Caution and controversy. Retrieved August 1, 2009, from www.library.illinois.edu/edx/rankings/rankoversy.html

Where Have All the Students Gone? Diversity and Recruitment Challenges in the Information Professions

Do not worry too much about your difficulties in mathematics. I can assure you that mine are still greater.

—Albert Einstein

At Zazzle.com (www.zazzle.com), aspiring clothing designers and fans of popular culture come together in a marketplace that fosters microcustomization. Microcustomization refers to the design and manufacturing of goods that do not depend upon mass production or mass marketing. With microcustomization, a designer can make a modest profit from selling a small number of unique items. A Zazzle.com user known as eMoney sells a line of clothing and accessories that he or she has labeled the "I hate math" product line. For instance, there is a plain white T-shirt with the words "I hate math" emblazoned on it in huge black letters and a keychain with the saying, "Innumeracy is a problem that affects 8 out of every 5 people." Fear and hatred of math has grown to become quite a cottage industry on the internet. There is a social group hosted at Tripod.com (ihatepi.tripod.com) called the I Hate Math Club, in which the founders, Justin and Shane, both high school students, describe their feelings about math:

> I mean, who really cares about how to factor a polynomial? "Will I be doing this in the future," you ask yourself? Most likely, no. The only jobs that may use this are teachers, mathematicians or some kind of job that requires extensive math! And anyone who would put themselves through that hell should seriously reconsider!

Attitudes toward math and specifically toward the specific topics of algebra, geometry, trigonometry, and calculus seem to be an important precursor to developing an interest in science, technology, and engineering majors and careers (Maple & Stage, 1991). Students who have a poor experience initially with math in elementary school or high school keep those bad feelings with them and generalize them into a belief that they will probably not enjoy or achieve competency in other areas that require some background in math. In Justin and Shane's words, "[S]ome kind of job that requires extensive math" includes many of the jobs in the information field that we have discussed in this book.

Early experiences in math class begin to influence student choices as soon as students have the discretion to select the courses they take, often by sophomore year in high school, but sometimes as early as elementary school (Ahuja, 1995). In their senior year, students who have already accomplished several basic math courses can also pursue advanced placement math. Those who accomplish an advanced placement math course during their senior year then have many additional options for college majors, including chemistry, physics, engineering, math, statistics, information technology, and other related majors. One of the students we interviewed, Maria, who was a college senior at the time, revealed the following essential formula:

> The funny thing in high school was that I didn't have a specific major in mind; I was undecided. However, since I love

> math, I like solving problems and solutions. My mom was aware of my strong background in science and math. So she was the one who advised me. She told me, "Engineering is a field that applies for the subject. So I know you're pretty strong at it." So, basically, I did my own research; I researched each field. And the one that attracted me more was civil engineering.

Maria did not recall having a particular major in mind during high school, but her capabilities with math (and science) allowed her to keep her options open. Later in the interview, she mentioned that she was a junior in high school when she "did her own research," and the results of that search led her to apply to colleges with strong engineering programs. The so-called accentuation proposition (Feldman & Newcomb, 1994) explains how students such as Maria begin making choices based on their own capabilities and the influences around them, such as teachers, mentors, and peers, and that these choices tend to reinforce themselves over time. A student in sixth grade who enjoys mathematics and has a teacher who encourages her to learn more about mathematics is more likely to choose a mathematics course if given the option as a high school student. Successful completion of a high school course gives a sense of self-efficacy that encourages selection of additional courses (e.g., an advanced placement course). Along the way, peers may reinforce her sense of achievement, and this in turn encourages deeper involvement in the subject. By the time she reaches college, the student has the ingredients needed to choose a major that requires math skills. At each point along the way, previous successes and encouragements accentuate the choices already made, and this accentuation directs the student down a path that is likely to produce additional personal "rewards."

The accentuation proposition also applies to courses in areas other than math and applies to student preferences as well as to their achievements. For example, in studying girls who took computer courses through high school, researcher Jane Margolis found what she called a "boy's club" effect (Margolis & Fisher, 2003). She found that when girls had early experiences with computers in which the activities and behavior of the people involved were male-dominated, the girls would begin to feel alienated from the topic. The more alienating, male-dominated experiences they had, the more the girls began to believe that computers were not for them. One girl said that she did not "dream in code" the way she believed boys did, and so she felt that computers were not a suitable area for her to pursue.

The accentuation proposition leads inexorably toward a situation in which students choose majors and later earn their degrees in areas where they feel most comfortable academically. Figure 14.1 shows a breakdown of undergraduate degrees obtained in the 2006–2007 academic year for four different groups of students: white males, black males, white females, and black females. The raw data came from the National Center for Educational Statistics (NCES; Table 285 from the 2008 Digest of Educational Statistics). *(Authors' note: We present just two ethnic groups to avoid making the graph too busy. Data for other ethnic groups show similar contrasts to whites and are available from the authors upon request.)* The percentages represent the proportion of students obtaining bachelor's degrees in a given major, accounting only for the majors shown in the figure. The complete dataset shows 1,524,092 students across 35 majors (some are groups of highly related majors) from universities in the U.S.

Note that we sorted the majors left to right according to their average popularity among women. Indeed, the most striking group differences in Figure 14.1 are actually by gender rather than ethnicity. The most popular major among all degree earners was business, although it was notably less popular for white women than for other groups. Women generally flocked more toward the health professions, education, and psychology. White women received degrees in education in much higher proportion than any other subgroup. Men were overrepresented compared with women in computer and information sciences, engineering, and physics. Black males and white males chose almost every major in equal proportions, but it is important to remember that black males are underrepresented overall in

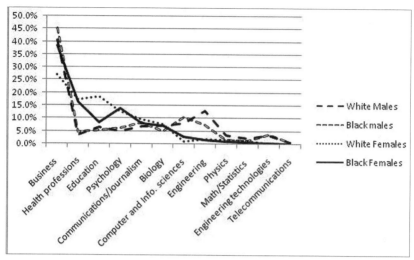

Figure 14.1 2006–2007 degree attainment of black and white students by gender across selected majors

U.S. colleges. For the majors represented here, there were 295,589 white male and 30,929 black male degree recipients (about a 10:1 ratio), as well as 377,580 white female and 60,297 black female degree recipients (about a 6:1 ratio). Miniscule percentages of students from all groups received degrees in telecommunications, engineering technologies, math or statistics, and physics. These majors were among the least popular across all of the possible areas of study within the U.S.

Now consider the popular conception of the necessary amount of math skill needed for these different majors (Osborne, Simon, & Collins, 2003). In the popular conception, most academic activities in business, the health professions, education, and psychology make little use of math skills. These majors are often seen popularly as "people" professions, with a substantial professional focus on interacting with others and a notable neglect of activities involving logic, geometry, trigonometry, calculus, or statistics. (Note that the popular view is wrong in several respects, most notably because psychologists and health providers often use and depend upon the use of statistics.)

Contrast these beliefs with the parallel set of ideas concerning computer and information science, engineering, physics, and telecommunications. Students see these areas as math intensive and lacking in human interaction. (While the former is undoubtedly true, the latter is not: Many academic and industry jobs relevant for these majors involve lots of interaction with other people.)

These beliefs about the kinds of educational background required for various professions, together with problems achieving a sense of self-efficacy in math, computing, or physical sciences, may cause some students to abandon any expectation that they can pursue a career in science, technology, or engineering once they have had an initial adverse experience with courses in these areas. As a basic steppingstone to keeping more of their technical career options open, high school students *must* have a positive and effective set of educational experiences with math and computing. Unfortunately, evidence from a large-scale international study suggests that secondary schools in the U.S. do not provide the kind of educational experience that generates this self-efficacy.

Every three years, the Organisation for Economic Co-operation and Development (OECD) conducts a massive international study of student achievement called PISA (Program for International Student Assessment). The 2006 study (the most recent available at this writing) focused on assessing science achievement, but it also included questions tapping into student capabilities in reading and mathematics. More than 400,000 students from dozens of different countries participated in the study. Judging by the overall results, if you were a 15-year-old high school student and wanted to get a good math and science education, the best places to live would be Finland, Canada, Japan, or New Zealand. U.S. students were ranked as low as 36 in math proficiency, well below our economic competitors such as Korea, the U.K., and Germany. The U.S. was also remarkable in its disparities: One in four students in the U.S. either barely reached or noticeably fell short of a minimum level of proficiency (level 1 or below). Nonetheless, the U.S. still had some high-proficiency students (level 5 and level 6), with about 9 percent of students achieving at these high levels, similar to higher ranked Ireland (9.4 percent) and Austria (10 percent) but still far short of Finland (20.9 percent) or Canada (14.4 percent).

If you were a student living in the U.S., you would generally perform much better at science and math if you were wealthy and went to a private school or a prosperous suburban school. In fact, one of the factors that set Finland, Canada, and other countries apart from the U.S. was that they had relatively little variation in the quality of education among schools. In contrast, the U.S. had huge variation among different schools, and much of that was related to the economic status of the students within those schools (in other words, whether the families in the community were generally rich or poor). These variations were confirmed in more recent assessments such as the National Science Board's biennial report (National Science Foundation, 2008, pp. 1-4–1-6). This report suggested that subgroup disparities in student preparedness and achievement start as early as kindergarten and persist or widen all the way through high school.

Part of the reason for differences in performance between schools stems from teacher shortages: Among the schools with teaching vacancies, three-quarters of them had vacancies in math and more than half of them had vacancies in science (figures for academic year 2003 were the most recent available). Between one-quarter and one-third of those understaffed schools reported having "great difficulty" in filling these positions. Math and science teachers also received an average salary of $43,000 per year, a paltry sum compared with jobs in the industry. Raises for math and science teachers between 1993 and 2003 were less than one-third of the raises obtained by people in industry with similar training. Trained math teachers chose their specialties based on their appreciation and enjoyment of the topic; it follows that they have the best chance of inspiring a similar appreciation in their students. When a school lacks trained math or science teachers, the opportunity for a student to achieve mastery and self-efficacy in these topics may decline.

A January 2008 report from the Higher Education Research Institute at the University of California, Los Angeles, showed that on a national level, four out of 10 high school graduates had failed to take enough relevant coursework to even consider taking a major in computer science or physical science.[1] A freshman in 1989 was half as likely to choose a science, technology, engineering, or mathematics major (about 6 percent of all college students) as a freshman was in 1969 (about 12 percent of all college students; Green, 1989). An April 2009 report by higher education policy analyst Tom Mortensen[2] suggested that these trends have continued from 1989 to the present, with overall declines in students choosing majors in mathematics, statistics, physical sciences, and engineering. There were slight improvements in biological sciences (a 0.7 percent increase in bachelor's degrees between 1971 and 2007) and psychology (a 1.4 percent increase).

At this point, the story seems to have emerged quite clearly: Positive initial experiences with math, science, and computing in school accentuate the likelihood of choosing more courses in these areas, which in turn facilitates choosing a science, technology, or engineering major in college. U.S. students who attend schools in poorer districts are less likely to have trained math and science teachers as instructors. Likewise, although girls have reached parity in math performance with boys, they are still more likely to see math as boring or irrelevant (Anderson, Lankshear, Timms, & Courtney, 2008). A lack of role models to guide them in noncoursework experiences, particularly in the home, also adversely affects girls' interests in math, science, or computing (Hyde & Mertz, 2009; Simpkins, Davis-Kean, & Eccles, 2006). Together these influences tend to result in fewer underrepresented minorities and fewer females completing advanced math and science coursework in high school. The final piece of the puzzle is the changing demographic composition of college students. Starting in 1982, more women earned college degrees than did men. By 2007, this trend had grown to the point that four women graduated from college for every three men. The student body in the U.S. has also become more ethnically diverse with increases in the numbers and percentages of African Americans, Hispanics, and other underrepresented minorities.

Historically, white males, who are nearly five times as likely to complete a degree in engineering as women, make up an ever-decreasing subgroup of all college students. The National Science Board reported that men earned 81 percent of the undergraduate degrees in engineering, 81 percent of the degrees in computer science, and 79 percent of the degrees in physics (National Science Foundation, 2010, p. 2-16; figures for 2007 were the most recent available). Among African Americans, Hispanic Americans, and Native Americans, only 1 percent to 2 percent planned to major in computer science as freshmen entering in 2006 (National Science Foundation, 2008, p. 2-18).

Although we don't necessarily need more technologists, scientists, and engineers in every possible job category, we clearly need greater overall participation by women and underrepresented minorities in many of these areas and particularly in the areas of study that feed into the information professions. At each step of the way, from elementary school to high school to college, an important part of the remedy lies in helping more students enjoy and achieve in math, science, and computing. Recruiting more female and minority students into the information fields and other technology-intensive areas becomes considerably easier when the pool of high school students who *can* choose these majors is larger. Enlarging this pool means having more students who have taken and *enjoyed* math, science, and computing classes in high school.

The National Council of Teachers of Mathematics[3] advocates the following important steps to ensuring that middle and high school students have mathematics instruction:

- A minimum of an hour of mathematics instruction each school day (many students now receive 40 minutes or less); students in middle school should not skip a semester of math in any given academic year; high school students should take at least one mathematics course per year, not counting any instruction specifically for helping students pass state assessments.

- All students, regardless of college or career plans, must learn algebra concepts and techniques from pre-K all the way through high school.

- Schools must provide professional development activities and retention programs that help keep math teachers in schools (most new teachers quit in five years or less).

- Math instructors must surpass state certification minimum requirements in their preparation to teach: Elementary school teachers should have taken at least three college math courses; middle school teachers should have at least minored in math; and high school teachers should have majored in math.

Similarly, in its position statements, the National Science Teachers Association recommends support for the deep college-level preparation for science teachers, professional development of science teachers while on the job, and coherent curricula that address scientific literacy for all students (www.nsta.org/about/positions/beyond2000.aspx).

We agree that these are worthy goals, and these national groups with a primary mission of advocacy are right to highlight them, given that funding and policy improvements at the state and federal levels can address each goal. We also feel, however, that these goals offer incremental improvements within established systems of instruction. Innovative thinking and local action offer additional possibilities for revolutionizing the way students experience math and science learning. In particular, all of the opinions we heard from students and many studies from the research literature converge on the importance of helping students achieve early and sustained enthusiasm for math, science, and computing.

Enthusiasm starts at home. Every parent has a responsibility to awaken a child's natural curiosity and interest in asking and answering questions about the natural world. Enjoyable scientific and math activities, readings, videos, and games are as close as the nearest public library. Parent involvement in school priorities and curriculum also makes a difference in what schools do and how effective they are at doing it (Epstein & Dauber, 1991; Lee, Smith, & Croninger, 1997). Relatedly, parents and teachers must work to improve the images that students have of science and technology. Our collective tax dollars support a program that appears on public television every week, a wonderful series called *Nova*, currently hosted by the charismatic African-American astrophysicist Neil deGrasse Tyson. The program paints science and scientists in a positive light; makes science, math, and computing understandable by many people; and is directed and produced in a way that is appealing for kids.

Making math and science relevant to students is an additional priority: Textbooks contain valuable facts, examples, and exercises, but math and science are all about changing the world and making it better. In the classroom, the tradition of having parents come in on career days to talk about what they do should provide opportunities for parents who work in engineering, technology, or a science field to have a direct impact on school-age students. This same model represents an additional opportunity for school partnerships with industry. Many university schools of business and management have perfected the process of bringing business practitioners into the undergraduate and graduate classrooms for the benefit of students; there is no obvious barrier to extending this model to other professions and down into high schools (or even elementary schools). Of course, the necessity for such external mentors is partly a function of the fact that teaching is so highly regulated and professionalized that the talents of science and engineering professionals who might be persuaded to teach are often unwelcome in the primary and secondary school environments.

The foregoing discussion highlights the importance of early classroom experiences, as well as mentoring, with respect to *preparing* a student for later success in these areas. But this preparation has an additional importance in making a wider range of choices available to students entering college. Many people who think about college enrollments and majors assume that the choice of major (and therefore the choice of profession) acts much the same as a marketplace, where students will flock toward the best opportunities for a stable future life (including a good, interesting, and well-paying job) and away from areas that offer fewer opportunities. However, this marketplace metaphor only works if students can truly choose freely among majors. Yet students do not feel that they have choices and in fact cannot freely choose a major in technology, engineering, or another technical area if they do not enter college with the requisite math, science, and computing literacy and if they have never had role models with whom they can identify and who exemplify achievement and success in these areas. Further, if the students' initial exposure to math and science courses left them with the belief that these topics were boring, irrelevant, or too difficult, then this also effectively limits their major choices in college. This book has declared that we need to educate more information professionals because the demand for the unique combinations of skills offered by these individuals will increase over coming years. Of course, no one can accurately predict the future, and the actual demand may be lower or higher than what we expect. Regardless of whether these professions expand at the rapid rate that we expect, however, we know right now that too few women and too few individuals from underrepresented groups choose to major in the allied fields of information technology, information science, computer science, and telecommunications. So we must work harder today to establish more balance and diversity in the information professions. If one positive side effect of this activity includes the recruitment of more students overall, that too will be beneficial. We can't say it any better than educational researchers Sue Maple and Francis Stage:

> It is important for women and minorities to achieve proportionate representation for two reasons. First, national reports indicate that educational pipelines feeding into quantitative fields show declines for all groups at a time when society is marked by advancing technology and an increasing need for workers with background in science and mathematics. One way to counter such declines is for women and minorities to achieve parity in their share of

quantitative degrees with respect to the population base. Secondly, occupational and economic rewards are not just a function of years of schooling, but of the major fields that students pursue. One way for women and minorities to close occupational and earning gaps in comparison with white males is to make gains in key fields (i.e., quantitatively based disciplines) where they have been underrepresented. (1991, p. 38)

We wholeheartedly endorse this sentiment. In the next and final chapter of this book, we take this call for greater representation of women and underrepresented minorities, gather it together with the other issues raised in this book, and make a set of practical recommendations for readers that we believe can help to attract more individuals of all backgrounds to the information professions.

Endnotes

1. Higher Education Research Institute at UCLA, "The American Freshman: Forty-Year Trends: 1966–2006," www.heri.ucla.edu/PDFs/pubs/briefs/40yrTrendsResearchBrief.pdf (accessed January 15, 2010).

2. Postsecondary Education Opportunity, "What Students Study in College, 1996 to 2008," www.postsecondary.org/last12/202_409pg1_24.pdf (accessed January 15, 2010).

3. National Council of Teachers of Mathematics, "Position Statements," ww.nctm.org/about/content.aspx?id=6330 (accessed January 15, 2010).

References

Ahuja, M. K. (April 6–8, 1995). *Information technology and the gender factor.* Paper presented at the ACM SIGCPR, Nashville, TN.

Anderson, N., Lankshear, C., Timms, C., & Courtney, L. (2008). "Because it's boring, irrelevant and I don't like computers": Why high school girls avoid professionally-oriented ICT subjects. *Computers & Education, 50*(4), 1304–1318.

Epstein, J. L., & Dauber, S. L. (1991). School programs and teacher practices of parent involvement in inner-city elementary and middle schools. *The Elementary School Journal*, 289–305.

Feldman, K. A., & Newcomb, T. M. (1994). *The impact of college on students.* New Brunswick, NJ: Transaction Publishers.

Green, K. C. (1989). A profile of undergraduates in the sciences. *American Scientist, 77*(5), 475–480.

Hyde, J. S., & Mertz, J. E. (2009). Gender, culture, and mathematics performance. *Proceedings of the National Academy of Sciences, 106*(22), 8801.

Lee, V. E., Smith, J. B., & Croninger, R. G. (1997). How high school organization influences the equitable distribution of learning in mathematics and science. *Sociology of Education,* 128–150.

Maple, S. A., & Stage, F. K. (1991). Influences on the choice of math/science major by gender and ethnicity. *American Educational Research Journal, 28*(1), 37.

Margolis, J., & Fisher, A. (2003). *Unlocking the clubhouse: Women in computing.* Cambridge, MA: The MIT Press.

Osborne, J., Simon, S., & Collins, S. (2003). Attitudes towards science: A review of the literature and its implications. *International Journal of Science Education, 25*(9), 1049–1079.

National Science Foundation. (2008). *Science and engineering indicators 2008* (Vol. 1). Retrieved March 16, 2010, from www.nsf.gov/statistics/seind08

National Science Foundation. (2010). *Science and engineering indicators 2010* (Vol. 1). Retrieved May 13, 2010, from www.nsf.gov/statistics/seind10

Simpkins, S. D., Davis-Kean, P. E., & Eccles, J. S. (2006). Math and science motivation: A longitudinal examination of the links between choices and beliefs. *Developmental Psychology, 42*(1), 70–83.

What's Next?

*The illiterate of the future will not be the person who
cannot read. It will be the person who does not know
how to learn.*

—Alvin Toffler, futurist

A longtime 40-something friend, Michael, received a raw deal a few
years ago from a company where he had spent most of his professional career as a middle manager. After more than a decade of dedicated service in the sales and marketing division of a large national
telecommunications firm, Michael received a pink slip and was
escorted with his box of belongings to the front door, another victim
of the several waves of downsizing that had washed through the company over recent decades. Though he had always served his firm pro-
ductively, Michael also worked on tasks that many other people were
capable of performing. As is the norm in U.S. business, Michael was
"employee at will," meaning that he could leave the company anytime he wanted and likewise that the company could fire him at a
moment's notice, for any reason or no good reason. We'll never know
exactly why Michael's name was prioritized for the company's latest
downsizing program, but the main issue is that Michael's capabilities
were seen as ordinary, and his efforts were seen as expendable.

Some people might say that this is capitalism at work and that
Michael should be free to market himself to another company while
his company hires someone else whom it finds more productive.

Others might say that workers—even middle managers—should have more protection against the whims of their companies. Whichever position you take, it is certain that Michael's company at some point stopped viewing his mix of skills and knowledge as mission critical. Michael was not in the information field, so he did not have skills with databases or web development or metadata or any of the other specialties we have discussed in this book, and it is impossible to know whether he might have kept his job if he had possessed different skills. As Chapter 5 discussed, there is certainly a long history of outsourcing and offshoring, particularly of computer programmers, that has resulted in many stories similar to Michael's in the information technology field. Yet it is also tempting to imagine that if Michael had possessed the expertise in his area of the business together with a deep knowledge in one of the focus areas of the information professions, he might have been able to "reinvent himself" in a way that his company saw as indispensable. In other words, when an important problem is easy to solve, there are lots of workers available who can solve it. Companies begin to see these workers as interchangeable, and executives have little concern about finding a replacement worker if one leaves or is let go. Good managers are also always on the lookout for ways of reducing the cost of frequently performed tasks. As we described in Chapters 4 and 5, when tasks become routine enough that they can be done more cheaply by someone else's workers or by a newly invented piece of technology, most companies look for ways of outsourcing or automating them. But if an important problem is hard to solve and only a few people in the region or the country have the unique mixture of skills and knowledge needed to solve it, those people will be in demand, and if they already have jobs, their companies will work hard to keep them on board, happy, and well paid.

Thus, a key message that we have been trying to communicate in this book, and particularly in Chapter 5, is that graduates can succeed in the workplace if they bring in a combination of deep knowledge in one area with broad knowledge in another. The deep knowledge may be in information, as would be the case for information professionals, or it may be in another area, as would be the case for engineers or business professionals or healthcare professionals. People who major in the information professions have deep knowledge in the area of their major: They should try to complement that area with broad knowledge of something else, such as psychology, biology, engineering, finance, statistics, or economics. People who major in psychology, biology, or another one of these topics should seek a broad knowledge of information and information technology (IT). As we discussed in Chapter 3, many, if not all, of the current sectors where people work have a high level of dependence on information and information technology to accomplish their jobs. The internet and its associated technologies have become the informational substrate of many activities across a wide range of professions. Few people who witnessed the early years of the network revolution in the 1970s and 1980s truly anticipated the impact of the internet on so many different aspects of our society. Even the most insightful futurists could not foresee how the internet would shape the processes involved in creating new knowledge and organizing existing knowledge. Businesses, governments, educational institutions, and the military all depend upon databases, image collections, digital libraries, and other large, complex information resources. In addition to these information resources, the most innovative research, engineering, manufacturing, and transportation activities in society now depend upon networking and telecommunications infrastructure that facilitates geographically distributed work and networked communities of workers.

For these reasons, information is in effect a new kind of required literacy, much the same as reading, writing, and arithmetic, which almost everyone must understand at a basic level and that some need to understand at a deeper level. We take for granted that most people need to have some understanding of math, even if they have no intention of becoming mathematicians. Likewise, everyone needs to be able to read and write, even if many will never write a novel or a textbook. In the same way, everyone needs basic information literacy: knowledge of the essential challenges involved in managing and processing information and how technology helps to solve those problems. Additionally, some need to go much deeper than a basic literacy: These are the information professionals that the world needs in order to develop, innovate, and sustain the massive information infrastructure that underlies more and more of the basic operations of society.

Joining the information field as one of these professionals carries many challenges. As we discussed in Chapters 7 and 9, the information fields also require a steadfast attitude of lifelong learning and constant self re-education because of the acceleration of technological change. The human-made artifacts of the profession (devices, algorithms, software, and standards) are in an accelerating process of evolution. Gains in computing power, storage, transmission bandwidth, and other fundamental building blocks of cyberinfrastructure constantly rebalance the trade-off between cost and performance. The rapid pace of development of information infrastructure implies that only individuals who dedicate their professional lives to self-education can truly keep up.

As an additional challenge, many negative stereotypes surround the information professions. From the negative stereotype of the antisocial geek who dwells in a cubicle to that of the meek librarian who stands behind the circulation desk, people in the information professions are the butt of much public misunderstanding and scorn. For those who do not fit the ethnic and gender profile of the majority of workers in their chosen field, both blending in and standing out can be uncomfortable and difficult processes. There is no way around the fact that most IT experts are white males or that most school librarians are females or that relatively few men and women of color have risen into the ranks of the chief information officers (CIOs) and chief technology officers (CTOs). Students who attend underserved schools in primary school or high school face the additional challenges of limited access to technology and limited availability of expert teachers and role models.

Despite these challenges, however, as Chapter 10 suggested, the information professions are in the midst of a transformational process of occupational culture. In the future, women and men from every background will populate the wide range of crucial jobs in the field. The cult of jargon and technical expertise will yield to the interdisciplinary challenges of working with complex cyberinfrastructure to reveal the essential character of the information professions as *helping* professions: not helping people with health problems, as doctors and nurses do, but helping people in other professions solve problems as information users. This new breed of information professional will possess both the capabilities to innovate with current information infrastructure and the brainpower to master new information infrastructure as it emerges. In this view, an information professional becomes a vital member of an enterprise who works closely with other experts to identify computing tools, data sets, and other resources that can be integrated to pursue any important objective in society: improving the environment, lowering healthcare costs, raising crop yields, curing diseases, resolving political disputes, or providing better education for young people.

These new information professionals must excel at the three I's: information, infrastructure, and improvisation. They must have the research skills to discover the needs of information users, and they must adapt available technology to satisfy those needs. They must forge the links among people, information, and tools in order to expose, mine, and process the mountains of data that are continuously generated by our societies. They must create information systems to integrate the communication, collaboration, and data management facilities that different communities need to form productive professional relationships. Information professionals must understand the importance of other professionals' expertise and work with scientists to represent, organize, and locate information resources. They must understand technology adoption and use, as well as the importance of user-centered design approaches.

The key to creating this new cadre of interdisciplinary information professionals lies in education and the connected processes of providing role models, mentoring, and creating safe, engaging environments for experimentation and exploration. To start on the path of becoming an information professional, young students need no more than a computer with an internet connection and a knowledgeable and willing adult to guide them through the forest of opportunities (and pitfalls) that exist. For instance, anyone who is not a professional game designer should try Scratch (www.scratch.mit.edu), an interactive, web-enabled environment that lets even the most inexperienced users build their own game with graphics and sound. Behind the fun of activities such as Scratch and similar activities such as Alice (www.alice.org), ROBLOX (www.roblox.com), and Greenfoot (www.greenfoot.org) lie opportunities for people of all ages to absorb an essential understanding of how IT is built and how it works. To continue on the path toward a career in information, older students should take courses in math and science, as well as continue their experimentation with information technology and the internet. As Chapters 12 and 13 suggested, the information professions are part of the so-called STEM disciplines (STEM stands for science, technology, engineering, and mathematics). A college major in any of the STEM disciplines, including information science, information technology, information systems, computer science, or telecommunications, requires solid skills in mathematics through precalculus (some, but not all, majors require some exposure to calculus). High school coursework in physical sciences (e.g., chemistry and physics) can provide the right ingredients to major in one of the areas of the information fields that is more focused on technology, while taking coursework in life science (e.g., biology, environmental science) can set the stage for a dual major or interdisciplinary major in college that provides a unique one-two punch of complementary skills in distinctive areas. Any science course in any area can provide important foundations in logical, systematic thinking that are essential for a major and a career in any STEM area.

According to the Hankamer School of Business at Baylor University,[1] "If you like new technology like iPhones, iPods, and Facebook, you have what it takes to major in information systems." This friendly statement tries to link the common current interests of many high school and college students in social media with the ability to thrive and succeed with a career in information, but we feel that it does a disservice to both users of these technologies and the people who create them. Users of technologies such as MP3 players like the convenience, power, or enjoyment that goes with using the technology, but they may not have any interest in the development, creation, or commercialization of these products. Just as taking an aspirin does not equate with wanting to be a doctor and driving down the street does not equate with wanting to be a highway engineer, merely using IT is not a powerful qualification for an authentic interest in the information professions. If a student is curious about how MP3 players work, how they serve as products in a profitable business, or how governments regulate the copyrights on music, then one of these interests may serve as a useful driver to pursuing a career in the information field.

And therein lies an important problem in recruiting a new generation of information professionals. Students of all ages and backgrounds, but particularly female students and minority students, often do not have mentors and role models to spark that flame of curiosity that changes the question of "What's on TV?" to "How does that TV work?" Give a student a computer game, and you have given her a few hours of fun. Get a student interested in how she can create her own computer game, and you may have launched a lifelong interest in technology, information, engineering, mathematics, or computer science. It was no accident that our interviewees in Chapters 6 and 8 frequently referred to a family member, often a father, who had originally piqued their interest in computers. Partly because of the negative stereotypes about geeks and nerds, there are few positive, public role models for the information professions in the movies, on television, or in the news. Try to think back to the last time you saw a heroic librarian depicted in a movie or a valiant, suave, handsome, and sociable computer programmer depicted anywhere. The absence of public role models, at least for the present, means that many, if not most, students have a huge gap in their understanding of what information professionals do and the importance, value, and benefits of their work to society as a whole. This gap has to get filled by parents, teachers, guidance counselors, public libraries, and other reliable information sources. The process has to start at the youngest possible age and go all the way through graduation from college.

In the next few paragraphs, we describe virtually everything that parents, teachers, and others need to know about student preparation for careers in the information professions. This is our teaching and learning recipe for up-and-coming information experts. We base our recipe partly on O*NET (online.onetcenter.org), the U.S. Department of Labor's comprehensive resource for information about occupations, and partly on information we obtained from our research participants with expertise in educating the information generation. Based on a systematic job analysis process, O*NET provides a huge database of job descriptions, along with a collection of information resources for each job, including skills, abilities, activities, tools, and technology (McCloy et al., 1999; Wagner & Harvey, 2004). Although there is no job called *information professional*, there are many existing jobs that exemplify the future information professionals we envision. In particular, we examined the skills and tools of seven different jobs, such as computer systems analysts, database administrators, archivists, and multimedia (audiovisual collections) specialists. The results of this analysis, summarized in Table 15.1, showed a striking degree of commonality in knowledge, skills, and tools.

The columns in Table 15.1 represent common distinctions in job analysis: Knowledge is anything that can be learned from a book; skills are usually learned through imitation, apprenticeship, and practice; and tools are any artifacts (computers or software applications) with which a job holder must have working familiarity. As Table 15.1 suggests, basic literacy, numeracy, and technology capabilities are fundamental to all of these jobs, as they are for many professional positions. However, it is interesting to see the importance of a group of interrelated skills and knowledge that pertain to working with the information users that these job roles often serve. Notably, jobs in the information professions depend heavily on the skills of active listening, customer service, teaching/training, and active learning. At some

Table 15.1 Knowledge, Skills, and Tools/Technology Shared Across Seven Information Jobs

Requirement	Knowledge	Skills	Tools/Technology
All Information Jobs Require These	Knowledge of a native language; knowledge of computers and electronics; knowledge of customer and personal service	Comprehension of written materials; active learning skills; active listening skills	Familiarity with desktop, laptop, and notebook computers; familiarity with database management software
Many Information Jobs Require These	Knowledge of essential science and math concepts; knowledge of administration and management of people and organizations; knowledge of how to train other people	Critical thinking skills; instructing/teaching skills; written communication skills	Familiarity with software development tools; familiarity with large or specialized computer systems; familiarity with metadata management tools

point in their careers, nearly every information professional will be in the role of eliciting requirements of information users and translating those requirements into effective systems and/or services.

With respect to tools, all information professionals must have a working familiarity of the most common types of computer systems, while some professionals may also need exposure to more specialized systems, such as mainframes and telecommunications hardware. Although relatively few information professionals perform much actual computer programming, most should have a working familiarity with at least one tool that facilitates the creation of instructions for controlling information technology (e.g., scripting, macros, and so forth). Finally, the necessity of familiarity with metadata speaks to a fundamental task that nearly all information professionals are involved in: organizing information. Metadata is data about data. In its simplest form, think of the description of a book (title, author, etc.) that comes up when you search for something to take out of the library—that is metadata. Metadata is an essential ingredient in addressing and overcoming the information chaos and overload problems described in Chapter 2.

Take a look at one other aspect in Table 15.1: The descriptions of knowledge, skills, and tools are expressed at a very broad level. O*NET must cover a wide range of jobs with as small a collection of categories as possible. To obtain a more nuanced view of the knowledge, skills, and tools required for the CI-Facilitator role, we asked some of our research participants who were experts in the information sector to brainstorm more detailed information about these three categories. Table 15.2 displays the results of that effort.

Although our experts focused less on fundamental skills of literacy and numeracy than the O*NET analysis did, these lists of knowledge, skills, and tools provide additional details, particularly with respect to information technologies. Also noteworthy, the experts were adamant about the importance of math and science skills. As we have suggested throughout the book, an individual who solely had deep knowledge of IT would not be as valuable in the job market as one who also had knowledge in another area, such as science, engineering, or healthcare.

What is perhaps most striking about Tables 15.1 and 15.2 is their similarities with respect to the mixture of capabilities that a working professional must possess. Every information professional needs a balanced combination of people skills and technological skills. Unlike engineering or mathematics, in which a person might excel based purely on technical mastery, the information professions demand a well-rounded person who is great at working, collaborating, and innovating with other people *and* who is knowledgeable and skilled at using the technological tools of the information trade (networks, databases, the web, and so forth). The requirements of this combination demand an education that draws on several of the traditional areas of study, such as computing, social sciences, and mathematics, and then integrates them.

It is possible to get this kind of education. The three authors of this book are involved now in educating college students with these mixtures of knowledge and skills, and we encounter a few students every

Table 15.2 Knowledge, Skills, and Tools/Technology Suggested by Experts

Importance	Knowledge	Skills	Tools/Technology
Critical	Knowledge of science and mathematics; knowledge of how the internet and other networks operate; knowledge of human-computer interaction principles	Communication skills (oral and written); service skills (working with people, determining user needs); information skills (collecting and analyzing data, technical writing)	Database design tools; web development tools; computer system administration tools
Important	Knowledge of information regulation and policy issues (privacy, access control, intellectual property rights, licensing); scripting, query, and programming languages	Database design skills; cultural sensitivity skills; skills at working with people with disabilities	Specialized/large computing systems; collaboration tools

year who have been well prepared by their high school experiences to excel. Unfortunately, there are too few who are well prepared and even fewer who are both well prepared *and* have received the kind of guidance, mentoring, and information they need to understand the genuine attractions, rewards, and challenges of a career in the information professions. We need more students. To get more, we need students at every level to have experiences that may open the door for them. Some straightforward actions follow from these premises:

1. If you're the parent of a student, ask your student's teacher how much math and science coursework he or she can take. Ask whether computer courses are available. If the answer is not many—or worse yet, not any— ask why and then ask what you can do about it.

2. If you are a student, go to the library and ask what the librarian does. Ask the librarian if your class can take a tour of the library. Ask to see the information technology that the library has and ask who is in charge of the technology. Take out a book on careers in science and technology.

3. If you are part of a family who owns a computer, use the computer together as a family to do something creative. Gaming might be a place to start, but go beyond gaming. Start a family blog or picture gallery. Use Scratch or Alice to build a game or an animation. Take every opportunity to ask how something works and why people created it.

4. If you are a high school student, find out who is the best math teacher—not the easiest—and take whatever courses that teacher is offering. The same goes for science and computers. Enter and compete in science fairs or any other creative competitions that your school sponsors or offers. For summer jobs, babysitting can be fun and lifeguarding can be rewarding, but how about doing some entry-level work in the information systems department of a local company. Better yet, start your own web design company. Most important, don't waste your senior year in high school: Prepare yourself for better options in college majors by squeezing a few more math and science courses into your schedule.

5. If you own a company or are in a position to hire some students for the summer, bring them in to work on the company's information infrastructure. Have the summer workers compile databases, build webpages, research technology product options, or anything else that gets them working with information professionals in your firm.

6. If you are a high school student looking for colleges, consider some of the schools listed in Appendix C of this book. All of them have information-related programs that may fit some of your interests and abilities.

7. If you are a teacher or guidance counselor, read Chapters 6 through 9 of this book to obtain a detailed and accurate understanding of what people in the information professions do on the job. Anyone who communicates to a student that computer programming and engineering are the only two career options in this field has done a disservice to that student.

8. If you are a college student who has not yet finalized a program of study, consider a major, dual major, or minor in the information field. Innovative college students have started combining majors such as information and business, information and journalism, information and science, information and art, and dozens of other combinations to create a curriculum that will win hands down in the job marketplace.

9. If you currently work in IT or any other area in which negative stereotypes adversely affect the image of jobs in your profession, break the mold. Become a bungee jumping librarian or a rock star network technician. Hire someone for your department who doesn't look anything like you.

10. If you are anyone anywhere, search the internet for *information professionals* and read an article about some aspect of the information field that you never encountered before. Then tell a student or a parent about it.

Spread the word that information is not just for geeks anymore.

Endnotes

1. Hankamer School of Business at Baylor University home page, www.baylor.edu/business/mis (August 18, 2009).

References

McCloy, R., Waugh, G., Medsker, G., Wall, J., Rivkin, D., & Lewis, P. (1999). *Determining the occupational reinforcer patterns for O*NET occupational units.* Raleigh, NC: National Center for O*NET Development. Retrieved March 16, 2010, from www.onetcenter.org/dl_files/ORP.pdf

Wagner, T. A., & Harvey, R. J. (2004, April). *Job-component validation using CMQ and O*NET: Assessing the additivity assumption.* Paper presented at the annual conference of the Society for Industrial and Organizational Psychology, Chicago. Retrieved March 16, 2010, from harvey.psyc.vt.edu/Documents/2004siop_wagner_harvey.pdf

List of Exercises and Associated Discussion Points

Chapter 1

Exercise: Find out the status of employment in the information professions

Learning Goal: To learn up-to-date information on various job titles in the information professions in the context of overall U.S. employment by using a federal government website.

Instructions: Decide on a job title that you will explore, such as *computer systems analyst.* Visit the U.S. Department of Labor's Bureau of Labor Statistics website (www.bls.gov). Follow links to the Occupational Employment Statistics (OES) section. Examine current statistics on wages and unemployment for the job title you selected. Compare these statistics to those for another job outside the information professions (e.g., landscape architect).

Discussion Questions: What is the current job market like for the job title you selected? Based on your comparison of two jobs, which job would you rather have and why? How do these current labor statistics influence your views on Chapter 1? Is the chapter too pessimistic or too optimistic? What other information did you see on the BLS site that may be of interest?

Chapter 2

Exercise: Compare the visual search engine performance and user experience

Learning Goal: To see how search engines organize information differently

Instructions: Many people use Google to find information. However, there are many other search engines that use different strategies and display the results in a more visual way. Think of a topic that you are passionate about (e.g., scrapbooking, sports, music, games). Now try searching about your topic by using each of the different visual search engines in the list that follows. Make sure you use exactly the same *search string* (the list of words you type into the search box) for each:

- Viewzi (www.viewzi.com)

- Snap (www.snap.com)

- Middlespot.com (middlespot.com/search.php)

- Wolfram Alpha (www.wolframalpha.com)

- search-cube (www.search-cube.com)

Discussion Questions: How is the information organized differently and how does that affect your user experience? Based on your comparison of Google searching versus these visual search engines, which of them get you the information you want faster and why? Do you agree or disagree with Ray Kurzweil's estimation of the required amount of memorization needed in order to develop a new area of expertise? How do search engines change our requirements of mastery?

Chapter 3

Exercise: Find out about informatics programs

Learning Goal: To learn about where you could study informatics and what would you learn

Instructions: Choose a field of study from the following list that most closely matches your own interests: archival informatics, biodiversity informatics, business informatics, community informatics, health informatics, neuroinformatics, organizational informatics, social informatics, sports informatics, quantum informatics. Using a college search engine such as Peterson's (www.petersons.com), find at least one undergraduate or one graduate program that teaches a specific branch of informatics. Obtain a list of the required courses and the electives for that program.

Discussion Questions: How difficult is it to find these programs and how many are there? What kinds of skills are suggested for a career in a specific kind of informatics?

Chapter 4

Exercise: Think about open source software

Learning Goal: To expand your exposure to the pros and cons of open source software programs and to understand more about how open source software development teams work

Instructions: Try to remember the last software package you purchased or think about a commercial package (e.g., Microsoft Word) that is installed on a computer you use. See if there is an open source software program that does the same thing. Next, go to the Free Software Foundation's website (www.fsf.org) and read about the free software movement. Find out about the organization's current campaigns.

Discussion Questions: What is the motivation behind this movement? What's the difference between the open source movement and the free software movement? Describe one of the current controversies or debates. If you had time to contribute to something like OpenOffice.org (www.openoffice.org), what skills would you need in order to participate?

Chapter 5

Exercise: Determine how and why jobs are outsourced

Learning Goal: To explore the concepts of outsourcing and the T-shaped information professional

Instructions: Visit artist Harold Kaplan's website (www.rooftop pottery.com) or the site of an artist of your choice. Try to determine where the artist works, where he or she sells artwork, and any other details you can about how the artist makes a living.

Discussion Questions: In what unexpected ways does an artist's business rely on information technology? What aspects of this artist's work would be difficult to outsource and why? Could this artist outsource certain aspects of his or her operations in order to make a better living? If you pursued a career in the information professions, what could you learn from the way that the artist makes a living? When people talk about outsourcing, they often grumble about local people losing their jobs. List five positive aspects of outsourcing for you, your community, or the nation.

Chapter 6

Exercise: Discover the wide range of jobs in the information professions

Learning Goal: To locate unbiased information about information technology and computing careers

Instructions: Jobs in the information professions and computing share many of the same stereotypes. Visit the Association for Computing Machinery's website (www.acm.org) and see what it is doing to try to debunk stereotypes that might deter students from entering the field of computing (computingcareers.acm.org/? page_id=61). Next, view some of the videos related to information technology careers found at the Department of Labor's Career Voyages page (www.careervoyages.gov/infotech-videos.cfm).

Discussion Questions: Which of these two sites was more appealing to you and why? Based on what you have read so far, how realistic do you think these websites are about information careers? What do you notice about how various information technology-related career tracks are named? What is the difference between a computing career and an information technology career?

Chapter 7

Exercise: Learn about diversity in the information professions

Learning Goal: To learn about the activities and support of student diversity organizations

Instructions: Join the Facebook group for the Black and Latino Information Studies Support (BLISTS) student organization at Syracuse University's School for Information Studies. Also join one of the many Women in Technology groups that are available on Facebook. Read about the activities and concerns of these groups.

Discussion Questions: Describe what you would ask the members of one of these groups if you were to send them a message. In what ways do you think this kind of support organization would be helpful to students? What kinds of obstacles do students in these groups face? If you were to pursue a career in the information fields, what other type of interest group would you want to create or join?

Chapter 8

Exercise: Define information professionals

Learning Goal: To enhance understanding of the variety of jobs types that are included in the information professions

Instructions: ASIST calls itself "the Information Society for the Information Age." Visit the ASIST website (www.asis.org), find out what ASIST stands for, and then visit the Careers section. Sort through the current job listings to see what kinds of jobs are located under the ASIST umbrella. Find out how ASIST compares with the Association of Information Technology Professionals (AIPT; www.aitp.org).

Discussion Questions: What did you notice about the jobs listed? What kinds of jobs are most prevalent? What is the pay like for those jobs? Imagine you are interested in interviewing at an upcoming ASIST conference or an AITP conference. Which conference would you go to and why?

Chapter 9

Exercise: Learn about national support organizations

Learning Goal: To learn about organizations that are helping to increase women's and minorities' participation in the information professions

Instructions: Visit and explore the website for the National Center for Women and Information Technology (www.ncwit.org). Write down information about one resource that is available there to support women in the information technology field. Repeat this process at the websites for the National Society of Black Engineers (national.nsbe.org) and the American Indian Science and Engineering Society (www.aises.org). Finally, read some of the latest news about diversity in engineering and information careers at Diversity/Careers in Engineering and Information Technology (www.diversitycareers.com) and at the Black Caucus of the American Library Association (www.bcala.org).

Discussion Questions: What is your impression of the main obstacles that women and members of underrepresented minority groups currently face in the information professions? How effective do you think the efforts to improve the situation are and why? What do you think of the idea of having separate organizations, such as the American Indian Science and Engineering Society, for different ethnic or minority groups? What other kinds of support, besides those offered by professional groups, do women and members of underrepresented minority groups need to succeed in the information professions?

Chapter 10

Exercise: Uncover the truth about your career options

Learning Goal: To gain information about how to conduct accurate, self-guided research about careers

Instructions: Perform one or more of the following three activities:

1. Obtain and read a copy of the article "Career Myths and How to Debunk Them" by Olivia Crosby, published in fall 2005 in the U.S. Bureau of Labor Statistics magazine called *Occupational Outlook Quarterly*. At this writing, a copy was available at www.bls.gov/opub/ooq/2005/fall/art01.pdf.

2. Download and run the free O*NET Computerized Interest Profiler (www.onetcenter.org/CIP.html) and use it to discover a range of activities and occupations you might enjoy. Take note of your "Interest Profiler Results" for use in answering the discussion questions.

3. Use the internet to look up the RIASEC model of career interests developed by Dr. John Holland. Make sure to learn what RIASEC stands for and the definitions of each of the words in the acronym.

Discussion Questions: Based on the activity or activities you did, what do you think is a good personal strategy for finding a good career? Some people say that they are "looking for the perfect career." Why is or isn't this a sensible statement? After completing the exercise, how do you feel about the "fit" of your interests and abilities to careers in the information professions?

Chapter 11

Exercise: Explore the interactive presentation of information

Learning Goal: To appreciate the ease of access to powerful statistical information

Instructions: Go to the website for TED: Ideas Worth Spreading (www.ted.com) and search for Hans Rosling or Chris Jordan. View any of their TED lectures about the presentation of statistical data (about 20 minutes each).

Discussion Questions: How simple and easy is it for statistical information to be accessed and displayed these days? How do you think the lecturers relied on cyberinfrastructure to enable their work? Share the story of the lecture you viewed. What was the agenda behind the lecturer's presentation? Debate Jordan's idea that by understanding and feeling statistical information, we can define ourselves more effectively and make profound changes in our behavior.

Chapter 12

Exercise: Explore librarianship

Learning Goal: To increase your knowledge of contemporary librarianship and the range of jobs that librarians hold

Instructions: Many job titles exist for librarians and library workers. Go to the site Real Job Titles for Library and Information Science Professionals (michellemach.com/jobtitles/realjobs.html) and review and count the job titles. Watch this short clip on YouTube about Super Librarian (www.youtube.com/watch?v=Bu-TijjVs_g) and follow that with a quick review of the related videos. Finally, check out the Tattooed Ladies of the Texas Library Association (www.txla.org/temp/tattoo.html) and The Modified Librarian website (www.bmeworld.com/gailcat).

Discussion Questions: Among the library and library worker job titles you examined, which was the most surprising and why? What, if anything, surprised you in the list of library job titles? What do you think about Super Librarian, and is this a helpful way to promote library services and/or dispel myths about librarians? Why do you believe that the Tattooed Ladies and the Modified Librarian wanted to publicize their groups and activities on the internet?

Chapter 13

Exercise: Discover the iSchools

Learning Goal: To enhance your exposure to the iSchools

Instructions: Visit the iSchool Caucus website (www.ischools.org).

Discussion Questions: The website opens with the statement, "The Power to Transform Lives." What is so special about iSchools? Are there any surprises in the list of Members of the iCaucus? What is the mission of the iCaucus, and what specific things does it do to accomplish its task? What guidelines does an information-related school need to follow in order to be a part of this caucus? Could you see yourself at any of these schools? Why or why not?

Chapter 14

Exercise: Find the fun in math and science

Learning Goal: To consider what attracts students to math and science and what may discourage them

Instructions: Write a paragraph about your parents' role in encouraging or discouraging you from being interested in math and science. Then go to the *Nova* site (www.pbs.org/wgbh/nova), which explains that "*Nova* revolves around a simple premise: the world of science is exciting!" Pick a few of the most interesting ideas you find there to share in the discussion. While you're there, see what job openings are available at *Nova*.

Discussion Questions: Share a childhood experience of when you were encouraged or discouraged to learn about science, math, or computing. Who do you think was most influential over you when thinking about whether you feel suited for a career that requires math, science, or computing? If you were an elementary school teacher, what would you tell your students about math, science, and computing? Would you say anything different to boys and girls? If so, why? If not, why not?

Chapter 15

Exercise: Explore high schools with a focus on technology and innovation

Learning Goal: To learn about the "high tech high" movement

Instructions: Search for *high tech high* and review the top five pages listed. Pay special attention to the curriculum, and think about how it compares with your own high school experience. Note any interesting student projects you see.

Discussion Questions: What are the similarities and differences between a high tech high and your own high school experience? For students who might not otherwise have considered careers in technology or engineering, how do you think attending a high tech high might affect them? Share some of the highlights of the student projects you came across.

Suggestions for Additional Reading

For each chapter, we have selected books and articles (generally ones that we were able to access online at no charge) that readers may wish to explore for further information about the topic that chapter covers.

Chapter 1

Farr, Michael. *Top 100 Computer and Technical Careers: Your Complete Guidebook to Major Jobs in Many Fields at All Training Levels.* Indianapolis, IN: JIST Works, 2007.

Info Tech Employment, ed. *Information Technology Jobs in America 2010: Corporate and Government Career Guide.* New York: Info Tech Employment, 2009.

Kirk, Amanda. *Information Technology (Field Guides to Finding a New Career).* New York: Ferguson Publishing Company, 2009.

Stross, Randall. "Are the Glory Days Long Gone for I.T.?" *New York Times*, August 8, 2009. www.nytimes.com/2009/08/09/business/09digi.html (accessed August 15, 2009).

U.S. Department of Labor. *Occupational Outlook Handbook, 2010–11 Edition.* Washington, DC: Bureau of Labor Statistics, 2010.

Chapter 2

Berners-Lee, Tim. *Weaving the Web: The Original Design and Ultimate Destiny of the World Wide Web by Its Inventor.* With Mark Fischetti. San Francisco: Harper San Francisco, 1999.

Leydesdorff, Loet. *The Challenge of Scientometrics: The Development, Measurement, and Self-organization of Scientific Communications.* Parkland, FL: Universal Publishers, 2001.

Stallings, William. *Cryptography and Network Security: Principles and Practices.* 4th ed. Upper Saddle River, NJ: Pearson/Prentice Hall, 2006.

Chapter 3

Ceruzzi, Paul E. *A History of Modern Computing.* 2nd ed. Cambridge, MA: MIT Press, 2003.

Chapman, Glenn. "Internet Age Re-inventing Music Business: Bandwidth." *Brisbane Times*, August 29, 2009. news.brisbanetimes. com.au/breaking-news-technology/internet-age-reinventing-music-business-bandwidth-20090829-f32z.html (accessed September 4, 2009).

Kleinman, Sharon, ed. *Displacing Place: Mobile Communication in the Twenty-First Century.* New York: Peter Lang, 2007.

Robson, Barry and O. K. Baek. *The Engines of Hippocrates: From the Dawn of Medicine to Medical and Pharmaceutical Informatics.* New York: Wiley, 2009.

Surowiecki, James. *The Wisdom of Crowds: Why the Many Are Smarter Than the Few and How Collective Wisdom Shapes Business, Economies, Societies, and Nations.* New York: Doubleday, 2004.

Chapter 4

Arthur, W. Brian. *The Nature of Technology: What It Is and How It Evolves.* New York: Free Press, 2009.

Brashares, Ann. *Linus Torvalds: Software Rebel.* Brookfield, CT: Twenty-First Century Books, 2001.

Elliott, Margaret S., and Ken L. Kraemer. *Computerization Movements and Technology Diffusion: From Mainframes to Ubiquitous Computing.* Medford, NJ: Information Today, Inc., 2008.

Lindahl, Alex. "500,000 Projects on Scratch: A Programming Platform for Kids." College Mogul, August 10, 2009. www.collegemogul. com/content/500000-projects-scratch-programming-platform-kids (accessed September 4, 2009).

Weber, Steven. *The Success of Open Source*. Cambridge, MA: Harvard University Press, 2004.

Chapter 5

Carmel, Erran, and Paul Tjia. *Offshoring Information Technology: Sourcing and Outsourcing to a Global Workforce*. Cambridge, MA: Cambridge University Press, 2005.

Farrell, Diana. *Offshoring: Understanding the Emerging Global Labor Market*. Cambridge, MA: Harvard Business School, 2006.

Kunkle, Pamela. *The Elephant in the Boardroom: Is India Worth All the Trouble?* Charleston, SC: BookSurge Publishing, 2008.

Taylor, L. C. "Profs Now Outsourcing Marking to India." *Toronto Star*, April 30, 2010. www.thestar.com/news/world/article/802845--profs-now-outsourcing-marking-to-india (accessed May 19, 2010).

Upadhya, Carol, and A. R. Vasavi, eds. *In an Outpost of the Global Information Economy: Work and Workers in India's Outsourcing Industry*. Delhi: Routledge, 2007.

Chapter 6

Checkland, Peter, and Sue Holwell. *Information, Systems and Information Systems: Making Sense of the Field*. New York: Wiley, 1997.

Eberts, Marjorie, and Margaret Gisler. *Careers for Computer Buffs and Other Technological Types*. 3rd ed. New York: McGraw-Hill, 2006.

Pletka, Bob. *Educating the Net Generation: How to Engage Students in the 21st Century*. Santa Monica, CA: Santa Monica Press, 2007.

Trotta, Whitney. "Oshkosh Creates New Social Networking Major." *Badger Herald*, September 1, 2009. badgerherald.com/news/2009/ 09/01/oshkosh_creates_new_.php (accessed September 4, 2009).

Chapter 7

Adams, Tyrone L., and Stephen A. Smith. *Electronic Tribes: The Virtual Worlds of Geeks, Gamers, Shamans, and Scammers.* Austin: University of Texas Press, 2008.

Anderegg, David. (2007). *Nerds: Who They Are and Why We Need More of Them.* New York: Jeremy P. Tarcher/Penguin, 2007.

Kuhlman, Erin. "Parsons Recognized as One of the 'Most Admired Employers' for Diversity." Reuters, September 3, 2009. www.reuters. com/article/pressRelease/idUS224238+03-Sep-2009+BW2009 0903 (accessed September 4, 2009).

Chapter 8

Bogart, Lauren. "Money Available to Train for Healthcare IT Jobs." San Diego News Network, September 3, 2009. www.sdnn.com/san diego/2009-09-03/business-real-estate/jobs-careers-employment/ money-available-to-train-for-healthcare-it-jobs (accessed September 4, 2009).

Bowe, John, Marisa Bowe, and Sabin Streeter, eds. *Gig: Americans Talk About Their Jobs at the Turn of the Millennium.* New York: Crown, 2000.

Gordon, Rachel Singer. *What's the Alternative? Career Options for Librarians and Info Pros.* Medford, NJ: Information Today, Inc., 2008.

Chapter 9

Brown, Eric J., and William A. Yarberry. *The Effective CIO: How to Achieve Outstanding Success Through Strategic Alignment,*

Financial Management, and IT Governance. Boca Raton, FL: Auerbach Publications, 2008.

Cohoon, J. McGrath, and William Aspray, eds. *Women and Information Technology: Research on Underrepresentation.* Cambridge, MA: MIT Press, 2006.

Wortham, Jenna. "The Race to Be an Early Adopter of Technologies Goes Mainstream, a Survey Finds." *New York Times,* September 1, 2009. www.nytimes.com/2009/09/02/technology/02survey.html (accessed September 4, 2009).

Chapter 10

Bystydzienski, Jill M., and Sharon R. Bird, eds. *Removing Barriers: Women in Academic Science, Technology, Engineering, and Mathematics.* Bloomington: Indiana University Press, 2006.

Chipps, Sara J. "Geeks Gone Wild." *ServerWatch,* September 4, 2009. www.serverwatch.com/career/article.php/3837826/Geeks-Gone-Wild.htm (accessed September 4, 2009).

Tucker, Carrie. *I Love Geeks: The Official Handbook.* Avon, MA: Adams Media, 2009.

Chapter 11

Lamonte, T. SU Students Are Finalists for National College Entrepreneur Award. *The Post-Standard,* August 10, 2009. www.syracuse.com/today/index.ssf/2009/08/su_students_are_finalists_for.html (accessed September 4, 2009).

Lawson, Judith, Joanna Kroll, and Kelly Kowatch. *The University of Michigan School of Information Guide to Careers in Information.* New York: Neal-Schuman Publishers, 2010.

Chapter 12

Farkas, Meredith G. *Social Software in Libraries: Building Collaboration, Communication, and Community Online.* Medford, NJ: Information Today, Inc., 2007.

Gordon, Rachel Singer. *Information Tomorrow: Reflections on Technology and the Future of Public and Academic Libraries.* Medford, NJ: Information Today, Inc., 2007.

Kneale, Ruth. *You Don't Look Like a Librarian: Shattering Stereotypes and Creating Positive New Images in the Internet Age.* Medford, NJ: Information Today, Inc., 2009.

Leckie, Gloria J., and John E. Buschman, eds. *Information Technology in Librarianship: New Critical Approaches.* Westport, CT: Libraries Unlimited, 2008.

Miller, Joseph B. *Internet Technologies and Information Services.* Westport, CT: Libraries Unlimited, 2009.

Chapter 13

Carr, Jeffrey. *Inside Cyber Warfare: Mapping the Cyber Underworld.* Sebastopol, CA: O'Reilly Media, 2009.

"Constructing an Ocean-observing Cyberinfrastructure." Scientific Computing. www.scientificcomputing.com/news-HPC-Constructing-an-Ocean-observing-Cyberinfrastructure-090409.aspx (accessed September 4, 2009).

Ellisman, Mark H. "Cyberinfrastructure and the Future of Collaborative Work." *Issues in Science and Technology* 22, no. 1 (2005), 43–51.

Guest, Tim. *Second Lives: A Journey Through Virtual Worlds.* New York: Random House, 2008.

Chapter 14

Farmer, Lesley. *Teen Girls and Technology: What's the Problem, What's the Solution?* New York: Teachers College Press, 2008.

Katz, Richard N., ed. *The Tower and the Cloud: Higher Education in the Age of Cloud Computing.* Boulder, CO: EDUCAUSE, 2008.

Rispoli, Michael. "Female High Schoolers Targeted for Math, Science Degrees by N.J. Colleges." *Star-Ledger,* August 20, 2009. www.nj.com/news/index.ssf/2009/08/female_highschoolers_targeted.html (accessed September 4, 2009).

Chapter 15

Collins, Allan, and Richard Halverson. *Rethinking Education in the Age of Technology: The Digital Revolution and Schooling in America.* New York: Teachers College Press, 2009.

Nowotny, Helga. *Insatiable Curiosity: Innovation in a Fragile Future,* trans. Mitch Cohen. Cambridge, MA: MIT Press, 2008.

Palfrey, John, and Urs Gasser. *Born Digital: Understanding the First Generation of Digital Natives.* New York: Basic Books, 2008.

Rifkin, Jeremy. *The End of Work: The Decline of the Global Labor Force and the Dawn of the Post-Market Era.* New York: Jeremy P. Tarcher/Penguin, 2004.

Roth, Daniel. "Making Geeks Cool Could Reform Education." *Wired Magazine,* August 24, 2009. www.wired.com/culture/education/magazine/17-09/st_essay (accessed September 4, 2009).

Partial List of Universities With Degree Programs in the Information Field

Brigham Young University, Hawaii
Computer and Information Sciences
soc.byuh.edu

Carnegie Mellon University
Heinz College
School of Information Systems and Management
www.heinz.cmu.edu/school-of-information-systems-and-management/
    index.aspx

Cornell University
Information Science
www.infosci.cornell.edu

Dalhousie University
School of Information Management
sim.management.dal.ca

DePaul University
College of Computing and Digital Media
www.cdm.depaul.edu

Drexel University
College of Information Science and Technology
www.ischool.drexel.edu

The Florida State University
College of Communication and Information
cci.fsu.edu

Georgia Institute of Technology
College of Computing
www.cc.gatech.edu

Georgia Southern University
College of Information Technology
cit.georgiasouthern.edu

Humboldt-Universität zu Berlin
Berlin School of Library and Information Science
www.ibi.hu-berlin.de/forschung

Illinois State University
School of Information Technology
www.cast.ilstu.edu/itk

Indiana University, Bloomington
School of Informatics and Computing
www.informatics.indiana.edu
School of Library and Information Science
www.slis.indiana.edu

Juniata College
Department of Information Technology and Computer Science
juniata.edu/registrar/poes/informationtechnology.html

Keio University (Japan)
Graduate School of Science and Technology
www.gakuji.keio.ac.jp/academic/shingaku/booklet/information/st/
    en_index.html

Long Island University, C. W. Post Campus
Palmer School of Library and Information Science
www.liunet.edu/cwis/cwp/cics/palmer
College of Information and Computer Science
www.cwpost.liu.edu/cwis/cwp/cics/cics2.html

National University of Singapore
School of Computing
www.comp.nus.edu.sg

New Jersey Institute of Technology
Information Technology Program
it.njit.edu/academics/index.php
Information Systems (Graduate)
is.njit.edu/academics/graduate/msis/index.php

Northeastern University
College of Computer and Information Science
www.northeastern.edu/chooseccis

Pace University
Seidenberg School of Computer Science and Information Systems
www.pace.edu/page.cfm?doc_id=17476

The Pennsylvania State University
Information Sciences and Technology
bulletins.psu.edu/bulletins/bluebook/college_campus_details.
    cfm?id=29

Information Sciences and Technolgy (Graduate)
bulletins.psu.edu/bulletins/whitebook/graduate_degree_
    programs.cfm?letter=I&program=grad_ist.htm
Information Science (Graduate)
bulletins.psu.edu/bulletins/whitebook/graduate_degree_
    programs.cfm?letter=I&program=grad_in_sc.htm

Rensselaer Polytechnic Institute
Information Technology
www.rpi.edu/dept/IT/undergraduate/index.html
Information Technology (Graduate)
www.rpi.edu/dept/IT/graduate/index.html

Rochester Institute of Technology
B. Thomas Golisano College of Computing and Information
    Sciences
www.gccis.rit.edu
Information Sciences and Technologies
www.ist.rit.edu
Information Technology (Graduate)
www.rit.edu/emcs/ptgrad/grad/98.php3#overview

Royal School of Library and Information Science, Denmark
Library and Information Science
www.db.dk/english/education/mastersprogramme

Rutgers, the State University of New Jersey
School of Communication and Information
Information Technology and Informatics
comminfo.rutgers.edu/information-technology-and-informatics-
    major/program-information.html
Library and Information Science (Graduate)
comminfo.rutgers.edu/library-and-information-science/library-
    and-information-science-department.html

Singapore Management University
School of Information Systems
www.sis.smu.edu.sg

Southern Polytechnic State University
School of Computing and Software Engineering
www.spsu.edu/home/academics/computing.htm

State University of New York Institute of Technology
Information Design and Technology Program
www.idt.sunyit.edu

Syracuse University
School of Information Studies
www.ischool.syr.edu

TUI University
College of Information Systems
www.tuiu.edu/cis

United Arab Emirates University
College of Information Technology
cit.uaeu.ac.ae

University of Albany, State University of New York
College of Computing and Information
www.albany.edu/cci
Department of Information Studies
www.albany.edu/cci/informationstudies/index.shtml

University of Arkansas at Little Rock
Department of Information Science
technologize.ualr.edu/informationscience

The University of British Columbia
School of Library, Archival and Information Studies
www.slais.ubc.ca

University at Buffalo, State University of New York
Library and Information Studies
gse.buffalo.edu/lis

University of California, Berkeley
School of Information
www.ischool.berkeley.edu

University of California, Irvine
The Donald Bren School of Information and Computer Sciences
www.ics.uci.edu

University of California, Los Angeles
Graduate School of Education and Information Studies
www.gseis.ucla.edu

University of Colorado at Boulder
Telecommunications Program
itp.colorado.edu/node

University of Hawai'i at MÇnoa
Library and Information Science Program
www.hawaii.edu/lis

University of Illinois at Urbana–Champaign
Graduate School of Library and Information Science
www.lis.illinois.edu

The University of Iowa
Library and Information Science

www.uiowa.edu/admissions/graduate/programs/program-
   details/library-inf-sci-ma.html

University of Maryland
College of Information Studies
ischool.umd.edu

University of Maryland, Baltimore County
Department of Information Systems
www.is.umbc.edu

University of Michigan
School of Information
Master of Science in Information
www.si.umich.edu/msi

University of Nebraska at Omaha
College of Information Science and Technology
www.ist.unomaha.edu

University of Nevada, Las Vegas
School of Informatics
www.informatics.unlv.edu

The University of North Carolina at Chapel Hill
School of Information and Library Science
sils.unc.edu

The University of North Carolina at Charlotte
College of Computing and Informatics
cci.uncc.edu

University of North Texas
College of Information
www.ci.unt.edu/main

University of Pittsburgh
School of Information Sciences
www.ischool.pitt.edu/lis

University of Sheffield, England
Information Studies
www.sheffield.ac.uk/is

University of South Alabama
School of Computer and Information Sciences
www.southalabama.edu/graduateprograms/cis.html

The University of Texas at Austin
School of Information
www.ischool.utexas.edu

University of Toronto
The iSchool at Toronto
www.ischool.utoronto.ca

University of Washington
Information School
www.ischool.washington.edu

Virginia Tech
Master's of Information Technology
www.vtmit.vt.edu

Wuhan University, China
College of Information Management
w3.whu.edu.cn/en/foster/Colleges.htm

Websites of Interest for Jobseekers in the Information Professions

Jobs and Internships

American Library Association Job List, joblist.ala.org

CareerMarketplace, www.careermarketplace.com

CareerOneStop, www.jobbankinfo.org

ComputerJobs.com, www.computerjobs.com

Computerwork.com, www.computerwork.com

Computerworld IT Jobs, itjobs.computerworld.com/a/all-jobs/list

Developers.net, www.developers.net

Dice: The Career Hub for Tech Insiders, www.dice.com

EarthWeb: Career Development & Technical Information, www.earthweb.com

Hi-tech jobs in the Research Triangle, www.trianglejobs.com

Internet Jobs, www.internetjobs.com

JavaJobs.com, javajobs.com

JustTechJobs.com, www.justtechjobs.com

LISjobs.com, lisjobs.com

MonsterCollege, college.monster.com/?wt.mc_n=monstertrak

Odin Jobs, www.odinjobs.com

Tech-Centric, www.tech-centric.net

Techies, www.techies.com

Professional Associations Related to the Information Professions

American Library Association, www.ala.org

American Society for Information Science and Technology, www.asis.org

Association for Computing Machinery, www.acm.org

Association for Information Systems, www.aisnet.org

Association for Library and Information Science Education, www.alise.org

Association for Women in Computing, www.awc-hq.org

Association of Information Technology Professionals, www.aitp.org

Association of Internet Researchers, aoir.org

Computing Research Association, cra.org

IEEE Communications Society, www.comsoc.org

IEEE Computer Society, www.computer.org/pubs/computer/career/career.htm

Independent Computer Consultants Association, www.icca.org

Information Systems Security Association, www.issa.org

Institute for Certification of Computing Professionals, www.iccp.org

Intelligent Information Systems, www.renewal-iis.com

International Association for Computer Information Systems, www.iacis.org

International Federation of Library Associations and Institutions, www.ifla.org

Internet Society, www.isoc.org

iSchools Caucus, www.ischools.org

Library and Information Technology Association, www.ala.org/ala/mgrps/divs/lita/litahome.cfm

Public Library Association, www.pla.org

Society for Technical Communication, www.stc.org

Special Libraries Association, www.sla.org

System Administrators Guild, sageweb.sage.org

TechAmerica, www.techamerica.org

Codes of Ethics and Professional Practice

American Library Association Code of Ethics,
www.ala.org/ala/aboutala/offices/oif/statementspols/
codeofethics/codeethics.cfm

Association for Computing Machinery Code of Ethics,
www.acm.org/about/code-of-ethics

Association for Computing Machinery Software Engineering Codes
of Ethics and Professional Practice, www.acm.org/about/se-code

Association of Information Technology Professionals Code of Ethics,
www.aitp.org/organization/about/ethics/ethics.jsp

Institute for the Management of Information Systems (U.K.) Code of
Ethics, www.imis.org.uk/about/codeofethics

SAGE System Administrators' Code of Ethics, www.sage.org/ethics

About the Authors

Jeffrey M. Stanton, PhD (University of Connecticut, 1997) is associate dean for Research and Doctoral Programs in the School of Information Studies at Syracuse University. Dr. Stanton is the co-author, with Dr. Kathryn R. Stam, of *The Visible Employee: Using Workplace Monitoring and Surveillance to Protect Information Assets—Without Compromising Employee Privacy or Trust* (2009, Information Today, Inc.). In addition, Stanton has published 77 journal articles and book chapters and refereed conference papers on research topics at the crossroads of organizational behavior and technology. Dr. Stanton's research has been supported through grants and supplements from the National Science Foundation (NSF), including NSF's prestigious CAREER Award, as well as from the Society for Industrial and Organizational Psychology Research Foundation, Procter and Gamble, the National Society of Black Engineers, and the Institute of Museum and Library Services. Before starting in academia, Dr. Stanton was a software engineer in the professional audio and electronic publishing industries.

Indira R. Guzman, PhD (Syracuse University, 2006) is an associate professor of Management Information Systems and Business Administration at TUI University in Cypress, California, and senior research associate of the Information Technology Workforce (ITWF) project at Syracuse University's School of Information Studies. Dr. Guzman holds numerous degrees, including a doctorate in information science and technology and a master's degree in information management, both from Syracuse University, master's and bachelor's degrees in computer science engineering from the Polytechnic Institute of Donetsk, Ukraine, and advanced graduate studies in banking and finance from the Bolivian Catholic University, Bolivia. She received the prestigious Fulbright-LASPAU scholarship and NSF funding for her academic training as well as her research. Dr. Guzman's business and consulting experience includes more than a decade of work as network administrator and chief of the Information Systems Department at the Argentinean Nation's Bank and other international organizations. Her research in information studies focuses on the impact of information technologies in organizations and in society. She has also conducted research related to human resources in information systems, specifically the study of the occupational culture of information professionals; their organizational role, gender, and ethnic diversity in the field; and recruitment and retention issues. As a researcher in this field, her accomplishments include more than 30 academic presentations and publications. Her work has been published in journals such as *Information Technology and People, The DATA BASE for Advances in Information Systems, Human Resource Management, Women's Studies, Review of Management Innovation and Creativity, Journal of Digital Information,* and the *Latin American and Caribbean Journal of the Association of Information Systems.*

Kathryn R. Stam, PhD (Syracuse University, 1999) is an assistant professor of Anthropology at the SUNY Institute of Technology in Utica, New York. She also coordinates an online graduate program in Information Design and Technology. She has taught more than 25 different courses, most of them related to anthropology; cultural diversity; or the social, organizational, and ethical aspects of information technology. She earned her PhD in social science from Syracuse University's Maxwell School of Citizenship and Public Affairs. Following this, she completed a 3-year postdoctoral research position in the School of Information Studies at Syracuse University. Her main research interests focus on information technology, community health, cultural conservation, and ethnographic methods. She has also published a wide range of qualitative research, and her articles appear in the following journals: *Information Technology and People, The DATA BASE for Advances in Information Systems, Journal of Digital Information,* the *Heidelberg Journal of Religions on the Internet, Computers and Security,* the *Journal of Information Systems Education, Surveillance and Society, Health Education Research, Social Science and Medicine,* and the *World Health Forum.* She has received financial support for her research from the NSF and the State of New York/UUP Professional Development Committee. Her work has been presented at more than 20 professional conferences in the past six years. Her background also includes extensive experience learning, writing, and teaching about Thai and Lao culture. She worked in Thailand for more than 10 years as a translator, teacher, and program manager in the field of community health. She has completed follow-up studies of her research about married women and HIV/AIDS and has presented her work at the meetings of the American Anthropological Association and the Northeast Anthropological Association. She is currently working on a project to preserve rural Thai culture through the collection and digitization of Thai cremation volumes.

Index